An ‖|‖|‖|‖|‖ ve

The Civil War Diaries of
Benjamin Franklin Pierce
(14th New Hampshire Vol. Inf.)
And His Wife
Harriett Jane Goodwin Pierce

Sheila M. Cumberworth
and
Daniel V. Biles

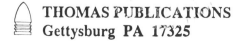

THOMAS PUBLICATIONS
Gettysburg PA 17325

Published by   THOMAS PUBLICATIONS
              P.O. Box 3031
              Gettysburg, Pa. 17325

ISBN-0-939631-71-7

Cover design by Ryan C. Stouch

*This book is dedicated to lovers,
of all times and places,
separated by war.*

TABLE OF CONTENTS

Photo Credits

Battles and Leaders of the Civil War - p. 66.

Daniel V. Biles - pp. 14, 20, 39, 40, 41 (bottom), 42 (bottom), 43, 44, 50, 55 (bottom), 56, 60 (bottom), 63 (bottom), 65 (bottom), 69, 84.

Bradford (NH) Historical Society - pp. 35, 38.

Sheila Cumberworth - pp. 2, 5, 25, 31, 41 (top), 42 (top), 47, 82, 83, 89, 90, 91.

U.S. Army Military History Institute, Carlisle Barracks, PA - pp. 8, 9, 10, 11, 13, 23, 28, 32, 49, 51, 52, 53, 55 (top), 56 (bottom), 58, 59, 60 (top), 63 (top), 65 (top), 68.

ACKNOWLEDGEMENTS

There are many persons without whom this book would not have been possible, or who have helped make this book much more than we ever thought it might become. We would like to thank the following people and institutions.

****

First and foremost, because this book never would have happened without you: Phyllis and Fred Lohrum (of Newport, Rhode Island) and Marianne Swenson and John D'Alessandro (of Natick, Massachusetts). Your friendship provided the contacts which proved to be the catalyst for us to make contact and bring this book into existence.

The New Hampshire Historical Society, Concord, New Hampshire was very cooperative in sending information about the 14th New Hampshire Volunteers.

We thank the wonderful citizens of Bradford, for all your hospitality and help. In particular, the Bradford Historical Society, Police Chief Al Grindle, Mrs. Veda Hosner, and Mrs. Betty Cilley, Mr. Parker McCartney, and Richard and Marcia Keller. The latter kindly hosted Dan in their home (on their old Pierce lands) in the Spring of 1992; Mr. Keller is president of the Bradford Historical Society.

The following libraries provided excellent resource information: Adams County Public Library, Gettysburg College Library, the United States Archives, and the United States Army Military History Institute at Carlisle Barracks, Pa.

We thank Thomas Publications for their willingness to undertake the venture of publishing this book, and especially Dean for his help, suggestions, and resources.

We thank Franklin and Harriett Pierce and their descendents, dead and living, for their commitment to preserving the family heritage from generation to generation. Those who do not know where they came from cannot know where they are going; it is the obligation of each generation to provide its descendents with a firm family tradition for living. We especially thank Joanne Murnane, Sheila's mother, for her enthusiastic support and contributions to this project.

Most of all, we thank our spouses and children, for bearing with us during this time of research and writing, so that this book could come to fruition.

The Authors
Sheila Cumberworth and Dan Biles

AN
ENDURING
LOVE

PROLOGUE

Minnesota's nickname is "The Land of 10,000 Lakes." It is a vast country of big sky and gentle hills, well suited for a youthful America. In spite of its legendary hard and unforgiving winters, it is a pleasant country—a country where generation upon generation of families are committed to stay, many in homes that are modernized versions of the original homesteads.

In the early 1950s two members of one such family of settlers, Joseph and Joanne Murnane, remodeled their family's homestead at Bald Eagle Lake, near the Twin Cities. The house had been built in the 1880s by Joanne Murnane's grandparents, Archie and Bertha Frances (Pierce) Thompson.

Remodeling the home was an extensive process which meant stripping the walls down to the original frame. Nothing could have prepared the Murnanes for the surprise that awaited them as they undertook this task. In one wall were numerous old newspapers, letters, and—most surprising—a set of seven diaries. All of these had been stuffed there decades before, perhaps in the dead of some frigid Minnesota winter for safe-keeping or even insulation, and then long forgotten.

Examination revealed that the diaries had been written by Benjamin Franklin Pierce and his wife, Harriett ("Hattie"), Joanne Murnane's great-grandparents. Written over the most tumultuous decade of American history, 1855-1865, the diaries were a record of Benjamin and Harriett Pierce during the Civil War. At that time Benjamin and his wife lived in Bradford, New Hampshire. Benjamin had enlisted in the 14th New Hampshire Infantry in 1862 and served until his discharge due to disability in 1865. Uncertain that mail would get through, both had kept diaries during our nation's great conflict to compare with each other once they were reunited after the war.

The discovery of the diaries initially created some excitement among the family, but as time passed they were nearly forgotten. The long years of harsh imprisonment in the walls of the house had not been kind to the diaries, as some of the entries done in pencil were virtually obliterated. Few bothered to carefully examine the diaries and read their contents in entirety. They were considered family mementos, curiosity pieces, but not much more.

Only now, some forty years later after their discovery, are their contents brought to light. The entries are brief, terse, and devoid of lengthy philosophizing on the great events of that era. These diaries were written by simple, common folk, not learned scholars given to philosophical reflection. But the Civil War was fought by such simple, common folk. People often view the Civil War in terms of the great battles, the grand movements of mighty armies, and the outstanding leaders of that era. But the war was fought and decided by the common soldier in the trenches—the "grunts," in modern military slang—with the support of ordinary civilians at home. It is the lives of these people, for whom the elemental needs of life were more pressing than the grand sweep of national policies and strategic campaigns, that

Benjamin Franklin Pierce and Harriet Jane Goodwin Pierce at the time of their wedding in 1855.

Franklin and Hattie's diaries reveal in their terse lines.

Brief as the diary entries are, taken as a whole their bits and pieces present a picture of the life of a soldier in the Union army and his wife back home during our nation's conflict. If the dairies are mundane in nature, they are mundane in a way which reflects life itself, for very little of our lives consist of the "mountaintop experiences" of high excitement and drama, but the everyday struggle for survival, the doing of the tasks at hand, and the maintenance of hope, commitment, and self-discipline against all the forces and events in life which would drive people to despair.

We have tried, in this book, to draw a picture from the material in the diaries of the lives of Franklin and Hattie Pierce during the Civil War. Piecing together the information from the diaries, oral family history, archival records, and written sources, we can trace Franklin's activity during the war: the places he went, the battles he fought in, his daily concerns for survival, the life of the average soldier in the army. We see Hattie's similar struggle on the home front as she tries to maintain her family on her own. In both we see their anxious struggle over the welfare of each other, even while apart and the fear of facing the future, not knowing when or if Franklin might fall in battle. Their joyful homecomings, their sad, pained departures, the "little joys" that brightened their days, their coping with tragedy: all these come to life on the pages of what they wrote. Yet through everything that happened, they did not despair, but carried on in faith, in hope, and in love. Their example is of love which "bears all things, believes all things, hopes all things, endures all things" (I Corinthians 13.9).

CHAPTER ONE

Enlistment and Muster-In

The summer of 1862 marked a turning point, if not on the battlefield, at least in the way both sides perceived the nature of the war and the objectives needed to achieve it. Over a year of inconclusive fighting had bloodied both sides, but left neither the North nearer to preserving the Union, nor the South closer to independence, than both had been at the war's inauguration in April of 1861. Costly engagements such as Shiloh, Tennessee, in April of 1862 and the Seven Day's Battle in Virginia two months later had dispelled the conviction that the war would be settled in one quick, bloodless battle. The war began with neither side prepared for battle; it continued with neither side prepared for the scale of casualties they would encounter in the months and years to come.

McClellan's defeat on the Virginia Peninsula forced a rethinking among Lincoln and his cabinet on their war objectives. They realized the South would not be convinced to give up its attempt at secession by merely one or two defeats on the battlefield. They knew now that the South would have to be conquered. More than this, the underlying cause of the war—the question of slavery and states' rights—could not be ignored. The institution would have to go if the war was truly to be won and the Union preserved. Any attempt to win the war, yet leave the institution of slavery intact, would only postpone, not end, the country's civil strife over this issue. The nation's sins for its evil of slavery, as Lincoln would note more than two years later in his second inaugural address, could only be atoned for through the blood of its sons and daughters.

A hundred miles to the south, Lincoln's counterparts in the Confederacy debated their own war strategy. The victory over McClellan in June had been very costly in men and materials; Jefferson Davis, Robert E. Lee, and others in the Confederate high command realized that they could ill-afford to continue the war on this basis. Sooner or later the North would win a war of attrition. Embodying the dictum of the great German military theorist Carl von Clauswitz that "war is the attainment of political objectives by means of force," the South embarked on a two-pronged course of action designed, not to conquer the North, but to break the political will of the Yankees to fight.

First, on the battlefield, the South launched its only concerted multi-front offensive of the war in the late summer of 1862. Lee moved on Pennsylvania through Maryland. In Kentucky, General Bragg moved towards the Ohio River. A smaller Confederate force counter-attacked the Union position at Corinth, Mississippi. In the space of three weeks, from Antietam on September 17 to Perryville on October 8, both prongs of this offensive were blunted. During early September 1862, however, they (rather than Pickett's charge at Gettysburg), marked the true high-water mark of the Confederacy. In retrospect, September

1862 was the closest point the Confederacy came to complete victory on the battlefield.

But as noted, military strategy was secondary to the greater political objectives: first, the Confederate thrusts in the east against Pennsylvania and in Kentucky towards the Ohio River were not aimed at acquiring territory. The Confederates sought to demoralize Union troops, putting such a scare into the Union citizens that their will to fight would be broken, thus encouraging Lincoln's opponents in their efforts to sue for peace. A successful campaign in Kentucky and Maryland might have persuaded those two border states, which were slave states under Union control, to enlist with the South. Moreover, by showing that it could defend its borders against Northern attack, first against McClellan in June and by carrying the war to the North in September, the Confederacy hoped to gain diplomatic recognition from England and France, thus pressuring Lincoln to end the Union blockade of Southern ports and seek a peaceful settlement to the war.

Such were the political and military situations in the summer of 1862. As the South prepared to go on the offensive, so did Lincoln and the North. The President issued a call for additional volunteers for the army: a nine-month enlistment of 300,000 troops. It was hoped that an army of that size could deliver the knockout blow against the South.

Men from all over the northern states, of all ages, rushed in a fervor of patriotism to enlist. Typically, a town meeting would be called to which citizens were encouraged to attend. In a form similar to religious revivals common at the time, patriotic speeches would be given, often with a testimonial from a person who had been in battle, followed by appeals to enlist. In New Hampshire, the last of that state's three-year regiments was created: the Fourteenth New Hampshire Volunteer Infantry. The men came from the towns and villages of the central and southwest counties of the Granite state. One company (company H) contained twelve pairs of brothers.[1]

Some twenty-five miles northwest of Concord, the state capital, lay the little town of Bradford. Nestled into a valley in the foothills of the Sunapee Mountains, Bradford was like many small New England towns: a crossroads settled by plain people who tried to scratch out a simple living from the land. The harshness of New Hampshire's climate required hardiness and determination out of those who settled there. The climate disciplined these traits into its sons who fought in the Civil War; it prepared them well for the challenges they would face. Four men from Bradford answered the call to arms and left home and family to serve the Union cause. One of them was thirty-year-old Benjamin Franklin Pierce, son of Nathan, Jr. and Abigail (Graves) Pierce.

As his name suggests, Benjamin Franklin Pierce was related to America's fourteenth President, Franklin Pierce. The Pierces of New Hampshire traced their ancestry to a Thomas Pierce, from Shropshire, England, who came to the New World in 1630, more than 200 years before Benjamin Franklin Pierce's birth. Settling first in Charlestown (now part of Boston), Thomas Pierce's descendants

4

Benjamin Franklin Pierce as a young man. The image is from a tiny tintype, about locket size.

moved to New Hampshire. The family was big and clannish, and possessed considerable political clout: besides Franklin Pierce, President of the United States from 1853-1857, the President's father had served two terms as governor of the state.

His mother's side provided Franklin with an ancestry well-accustomed to the rigors of war. Abigail Graves was a descendent of Scots who came to America in the mid-1700s. According to family records, their original surname was Graham; in Scotland they had been of noble lineage. Supporters of Bonnie Prince Charlie, they fled Scotland following Charles' defeat at Culloden Moor in 1746, changed their name to Graves for the sake of safety, and immigrated to America. As with many of their fellow country-folk from the border area of North Briton and South Scotland, they found the rugged hills and valleys of New Hampshire a reminder of their ancestral home. Here Abigail's ancestors settled, in the town of Suncook, near East Washington. The people of North Briton and Scotland and their descendants are the products of a culture forged in the furnace of centuries of continual warfare. It is a culture which imbues in its sons and daughters the values of sacrifice, esteem for the military arts, fierce personal loyalties, and endurance of hardship. All of these would serve Franklin Pierce well in the adventure his life undertook in late summer, 1862.

At the time of his enlistment, Franklin, or "Frank"—the "Benjamin" was not used, except formally—Pierce was a railroad engineer. He was married to the former Harriett Jane Goodwin. Her family roots were in Vermont, though Harriett's father had left Vermont for a new life in Indiana in the 1830s. Along the journey, in Ohio, Hattie was born in 1836. Franklin met Hattie and married her twenty years later in Terre Haute, Indiana. He had gone west to work on the building of the railroads; according to family history, Franklin drove the first engine across the Wabash River.

Following their marriage the couple returned to Bradford. By the summer of 1862 the Pierces had three children, all girls: Eva, born in 1856; Annie, born in 1858; and Bertha Frances (the great-grandmother of the authoress), born in 1861. It was indeed a tremendous step of faith and courage for a man to leave his civilian employment, wife, and three young children to go off to war. Why did he do it? An entry in Hattie's diary on election day two years later perhaps gives a hint of the motivations behind Pierce's sacrifice:

Nov. 8
This is a day of very great importance to the
country. I hope it will be decided in favor
of the Union and liberty.

To preserve the Union: this was the first, most important reason for going off to war. But more than just preserving the nation, the war sought to preserve an idea which was the basis and goal of the nation: liberty. The defense of liberty was the battle-cry which spurred families like Franklin and Hattie Pierce's to risk their lives

6

for its sake. What might Franklin and Hattie Pierce have understood by this term, "liberty?"

Of course, the South thought it was fighting for liberty, too: the freedom to uphold its way of life and rule over its own affairs, free from the dictates of a central government. Thus the common name in the South for the Civil War: "The War of Northern Aggression." The war was understood as an attempt by the North to impose its rule over the South; the South, therefore, had a legitimate right to self-defense of its freedom to rule itself.

Coming from the descendants of the Massachusetts Bay Colony, the Pierces understood freedom in a far different way. As in all New England, liberty was always understood as "ordered liberty." That is, New Englanders understood liberty as specific freedoms exercised within a particular order which people were bound to uphold. John Winthrop, one of the founders of the region, stated that civil or federal, or "moral" liberty, originated

> ...in reference to the covenant between God and man. It is a liberty to that only which is good, just, and honest. This liberty you are to stand for, with the hazard not only of your goods but of your lives if need be.... This liberty is maintained and exercised in a way of subjection to authority....[2]

For the Pierces, as for all New England (and, in truth, Lincoln), the "War of Southern Rebellion" was not the South's defense of its freedom, but rather its revolt against freedom, against the very ordering of society by which the "blessings of liberty" were secured.

Franklin's sentiments in favor of the war were also, no doubt, highly influenced by his mother. In a town which always voted heavily for Democrats well into the 20th century (including McClellan over Lincoln in 1864), Abigail was a strident abolitionist. A story recorded by one of her descendants recalls her strong abolitionist stance, as well as her character:

> Our great-grandmother, Abigail Graves, who became the wife of Nathan Pierce, seems to have been a woman of New England gumption. She was a school-teacher, probably in the vicinity of East Washington, New Hampshire, where the Graves family lived. In an era when it was an adventurous thing to do, she took a stage-coach trip to Boston, nearly a hundred miles away.
>
> She was a friend of Gov. Benjamin Franklin Pierce of New Hampshire and admired him so much that she named her only son, our grandfather, after him—also Benjamin Franklin Pierce.
>
> After her marriage to Nathan Pierce she lived on their farm at Bradford, New Hampshire. His brother, Cummings Pierce, owned a farm adjoining.
>
> As the question of slavery grew in importance, Great-grandmother Pierce became violently anti-slavery—an abolitionist. When Benjamin Franklin Pierce, the governor's son, was canvassing New Hampshire in his campaign for the Presidency, he passed her home. Because of his tolerance toward slavery and his attitude toward the South, Abigail Pierce refused to invite him into the house, or even to go out to his

7

carriage to speak to him. He drove on to the next farm to spend the night with Uncle Cummings Pierce, whom she always considered a copperhead.[3]

Franklin Pierce enlisted on August 22, 1862, as a private. Promised an enlistment bounty of $100, he received $25 upon reporting for duty, the remainder to be given on his discharge. Records indicate he was given $13 in advance.[4] At 30 years old, he was one of the elder statesmen in his company; interestingly, the oldest member in the regiment was 63. The youngest, one George Jones of the town of Washington, who undoubtedly lied about his age to enlist, was 15,[5] yet he was made a corporal upon mustering in.[6] Youth in general dominated the ranks of the Union army. Indeed, men 30 years or older comprised only 10% of the entire Union army, while 60% of the soldiers were twenty-four or younger.[7] By the standards of his day, Franklin Pierce was an old man fighting in a young man's war.

The 14th New Hampshire mustered in at Camp Cheshire, Concord beginning 19 September. Pierce arrived on the 24th, was assigned to Company I, and made (or possibly elected) a corporal. The company achieved notice from the start as a well-disciplined unit, quickly well-schooled in basic military drill. For this achievement, credit is due, not to the officer corps, but the sergeants in the company. A historian of the regiment later remarked on the company,

The colors of the 14th New Hampshire Volunteer Infantry, after the war.

Colonel Robert Wilson, first commander of the 14th New Hampshire.

    The non-commissioned officers of [Co.] I were very competent and reliable men; and in this respect the company ranked well up with D, G and other companies which were pre-eminent in their complement of subaltern officers. Concerning the election of company officers, there is room for the supposition that the ceremony of choosing the same was not perfectly satisfactory; and by some members of the company it was considered that no election at all was held for captain and second lieutenant, while the choice of first lieutenant was "a farse."[8]

These comments reflect what was typical in many regiments in the Union army in the initial years of the war. Lacking a large officer corps to start with, made even smaller by the loss of Southern officers to serve in the ranks of the Confederacy, the officers in many regiments were elected by the men themselves. They were, thus, often unschooled in military tactics; worse, many received their positions by virtue of their civilian status and wealth, whether or not they had any special aptitude for the job. Many officers were simply incompetent for their assignments, and it took several years of war for a more skilled officer corps to emerge. Thus, also, in many units the adage applied that "the sergeants are the backbone of the army."

The 14th Regiment stayed at Concord for almost a month. The men began learning the basic military drill which would be so necessary for effective maneuver and survival on the battlefield. This drill had to be mastered at all levels of the command, from platoon size up to the entire regiment. On the 18th of October the regiment departed for its first destination in its tour of duty: the defense of the nation's capital. Colonel Robert Wilson commanded the regiment, nine hundred and sixty-seven strong. For two hundred and twenty-six, it was the last time they would see their home and loved ones.[9]

SURG. W. H. THAYER.

ASST. SURG. M. PERKINS.

ASST. SURG. F. C. WEEKS.

ADJT. L. W. WRIGHT.

Q. M., WM. A. HEARD.

CHAPLAIN E. T. ROWE.

STAFF OFFICERS.

Staff Officers of the 14th New Hampshire.

CAPT. T. A. RIPLEY.

CAPT. N. L. CHANDLER.

CAPT. W. E. COBLEIGH.

LIEUT. COL. O. H. MARSTON.

LIEUT. A. F. HUSSEY.

LIEUT. D. H. PILLSBURY.

LIEUT. H. P. PAGE.

LIEUT. COL. AND LINE OFFICERS.

Line Officers of the 14th New Hampshire. Captain N. L. Chandler served for a time in Company I, Pierce's unit.

CHAPTER TWO

Defending Washington

Nestled among the rolling hills of central Maryland, thirty miles northwest of our nation's capital, is the little town of Poolesville. Settled in 1760, the town has remained a quiet little village for two hundred years. Though the town is about to experience the onslaught of suburbanization from Washington's expansion, a traveler to the area today would find the surrounding countryside not very changed from what it was like during the Civil War: Little towns separated by open areas of farmland.

Until the Civil War, Poolesville had been just a quiet little crossroads and farming community. The war changed all that; the area became a major training area and camp for Union troops. It was to this little village that Franklin Pierce and the 14th New Hampshire came in October of 1862. Leaving Concord on the 18th, the regiment reached Washington two days later. Their first campsite was in shelter tents on the east side of Capitol Hill. The regiment was attached to Grover's Independent Brigade, named for division commander General Cuvier Grover, under whose command they would remain for the rest of the war. By 5 January, according to Pierce's diary, the commander of the brigade itself was one Colonel Jewett, and the brigade was part of the 22nd Corps defending Washington. Besides the 14th New Hampshire, the brigade included the 39th Massachusetts, the 10th Vermont, the 23rd Maine, "Scott's 900 Cavalry," and the 10th Massachusetts Light Battery.[1] A few days later the regiment moved out to join its new assignment with the brigade at Poolesville.

By the second year of the war, Washington was the most heavily defended area on the continent. Bordering the Confederacy, only 100 miles from Richmond, located in a state with strong southern sympathies, the city was ringed by forts on all sides. Poolesville lay beyond this defense ring, but it was not an insignificant assignment. The town was no stranger to the sounds of battle. With the Potomac River only five miles away, Poolesville was often the site of skirmishes with rebel guerilla forces which crossed the river to raid for supplies and annoy or probe the Washington defenses. One year before, a sizeable Union force had left Poolesville and crossed the Potomac at what is now White's Ferry (then Conrad's Ferry), only to be repulsed by Confederate forces just across the river at the Battle of Ball's Bluff. One of the participants was a young Oliver Wendell Holmes, the future Supreme Court Justice, who would participate in many more campaigns during the war.

Just a month before Pierce's arrival with the 14th, Poolesville had been the site of a skirmish with elements of Lee's Army of Northern Virginia as they crossed the Potomac at White's Ferry in the drive which culminated with the Battle of Antietam. With Confederate forces just a few miles away on the other side of the

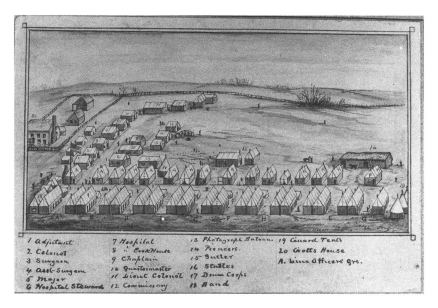

Camp of the 14th New Hampshire Infantry at Poolesville, Maryland, during the winter of 1862-63.

Potomac, Poolesville was not far from the front lines of the war in the East. Indeed, the sympathies of many citizens of the town lay with the South. One of their own, an ordained Baptist preacher by the name of Elijah White, became a colonel of a regiment under the command of the great southern cavalry commander, J.E.B. Stuart. On July 4, 1863, while the bulk of the armies were fighting at Gettysburg further north, White led a band of Confederate raiders into Poolesville against the detachment of soldiers—about 40 in all—who had been left to guard the town. At the time the entire garrison was attending services at the Presbyterian Church in town, White and his men surrounded the church, blockaded the single entrance door, and captured the garrison without a fight.[2]

Pierce's regiment had its first taste of battle, shortly after their arrival, in skirmishes which took place near the town in November and December. No casualties occurred in these engagements, but sporadic firefights did occur from time to time. One incident Pierce records was a clash between some Confederate cavalry raiding artillery units:

Tuesday, 6 January
Raining all the afternoon. Paymaster
came last night. Quite a sharp fight between
cavalry and Battery....

Another problem was snipers. In this area there were either Confederate soldiers

13

Above: The John Poole house, built by the early settler of Poolesville, John Poole in 1793. Originally a store, it was also a U. S. Post Office in the 1800s. Below: Main Street Poolesville today, looking east toward the town hall.

sneaking across the Potomac or local civilians friendly to the Confederate cause (Maryland was a slave state that had been placed under martial law by the Federal government at the start of the war):

<blockquote>

Monday, 9 March

Clear and cool. Went to town and got a
picture taken. Man in Co. H got shot while
after straw. Hit on the hand and through leg.
Didn't find the one that shot him.

</blockquote>

Sometimes the raiders or snipers were caught. Pierce records in his entry for Wednesday, 18 March being assigned prison guard duty, with "six prisoners there now."

But skirmishes with the enemy were the exception rather than the rule during the 14th's assignment at Poolesville. More common was the daily routine of camp life. The 14th Regiment from the Granite state settled in and made Poolesville their home for the six months. Their accommodations were spartan, but probably better than in many other sectors of the army. A note in his diary for 16 January, 1863, gives us an idea of the shelter Pierce and his comrades enjoyed, or at least bore with:

<blockquote>

Raining hard all night. Clears off about 9
O.c and turns cold toward night.... The old
stove smoked awfully. Cut a hole in the door
and put a piece of stove pipe in to give it a good draft.

</blockquote>

The entry reveals that within a few months after their arrival the regiment was housed in log, or log-and-tent, huts. The latter were more likely the case, as Pierce's entry for April 3 suggests that tent canvas made up at least part of their accommodations. These combinations of tents with log frames and wooden doors certainly were a vast improvement over sleeping in tents alone during winter weather. Each hut housed two to four soldiers. They slept, as Pierce's entry for 31 January indicates, in bunkbeds. The nearby countryside was soon stripped of trees to provide logs for the shelters, with mud daubed between the logs to provide protection against the wind. To provide additional protection against the elements, the floor was dug out several feet down. Each hut had a fireplace or, in Pierce's hut, a simple stove to provide heat.

Around the little village of Poolesville, then, an entire new town of these log huts sprung up to house the soldiers. Streets marked with imaginative names divided the camp into a rough gridwork. It was not a life of luxury by any means. With the poor hygienic and sanitary conditions of the day, camp life was crude, smelly, and dirty. Still, accommodations in the camps around Washington were better than in units further out in the field, and certainly more comfortable than in the Confederate camps just across the Potomac.

Just as shelter was spartan, so was the food. The standard daily ration for a Union soldier in the field was hardtack, salt pork, dried beans, and coffee. "Hardtack" was a thick, square, flour-and-water cracker that got its name from the difficulty men had in biting off a piece to eat. Rumor had it that hardtack was tough enough to stop a bullet. Often spoiled by the time it arrived to the soldiers, many times it was softened by soaking it in water, then frying it in pork fat. Coffee was consumed in great quantity, made whenever the soldiers got a free moment to make it. Rations were distributed as whole beans which the soldiers ground with the butt of their rifles, then boiled right in the cup.

During his time at Poolesville, however, Pierce and his fellow soldiers in the 14th New Hampshire enjoyed a much more healthy and varied diet. They enjoyed an ample supply of beef and potatoes in addition to hardtack. From his 1863 diary:

Tuesday, 13 January
Had some fresh beef for dinner fryd.

****

Wednesday, 14 January
Had some liver for breakfast.

****

Friday, 16 January
Had some fryd potatoe for super.

****

Wednesday, 21 January
Had some beef steak for dinner.

[Beef was apparently plentiful, a few days later his diary notes that he drew a fresh supply of beef for his company. This and other entries reveals that one of Pierce's duties was drawing supplies for his company.]

****

Monday, 23 March
Had stewed beans for dinner.

Pierce's situation was not unusual; the closer troops were stationed to Washington, the better they were supplied. When, in the summer of 1864, Grant pulled units off the Washington defenses to assist him in his campaign against Lee, the battle-hardened troops in the Army of the Potomac delighted in ridiculing the new troops on the front for being overweight and spoiled.

Still, the lack of both quantity and quality in rations did much to undermine the health of many a soldier and assist the devastating impact disease had upon the camps. Wars always assist in the transmission of disease; soldiers come from all different parts of a country and are suddenly exposed to bacteria and viruses not common to them back home. It was no different in the Civil War. In addition, in large part due to simple ignorance about proper hygiene and disease prevention, sanitary conditions in the camps were anything but healthy. There were no consistent, standard practices for proper waste and sewage disposal.

Under such conditions, diseases spread like wildfire. Mosquitos, fleas, lice, and flies infested the camps, spreading illness with them. Dysentery, due in large part to the use of impure, unboiled water, was a common affliction of almost every soldier. In Union army units, cases ran from 60% to over 90% of troop strength.[3]

Other diseases also flourished. Typhoid fever, also known as "camp fever," was a deadly killer. It resulted from contaminated water, milk, or food. In the summer, malaria often afflicted the soldiers; though at the time they did not know that the disease was born by mosquitoes, they did know that quinine provided relief from the illness. Lice spread typhus. These diseases were not new to the Chesapeake Bay region; they were in fact the causes of mortality which had afflicted people since colonists had first come to the area.[4] This is reflected in the official report of the 14th New Hampshire; almost all of the deaths by disease listed in it are those of the Chesapeake region: Typhoid, malaria, dysentery.

Venereal disease was also rampant among troops, occurring at a rate of over 8%. It was not surprising: The troops received a steady entertainment of "horizontal refreshment," as it was called, from the many practitioners of the world's "oldest profession" who followed the troops wherever the armies marched and fought. Washington, D. C. was as much the nation's brothel capital as it was the seat of government. Some suspect the term "hooker" for prostitute came from the nickname of Union General Joseph Hooker, whose bad reputation for women and whiskey was known on both sides.[5]

Disease was no stranger in the camp of the 14th New Hampshire during its months at Poolesville. The first camp death due to disease was one of Pierce's own acquaintances from Bradford. He notes in his diary on January 27, 1863: "E.O. Marshall died last night at 10 O.c." This was Eugene O. Marshall, who died of typhoid. He was a farmer, just 18 years old. The next day his entry records that Marshall's body was taken to Washington by two sergeants, Henry Paul and Ransom Huntoon, where it was shipped home for burial in Bradford.[6] Three weeks later Pierce records that two more men died from disease: Philander Peck, a twenty-year old farmer from Newport, and Elias Powers, age 18, a farmer from Croydon. Again typhoid was the culprit.[7] On March 23 Pierce records that his 2nd Lieutenant, a 26-year old farmer from Grantham by the name of D. J. Pillsbury, came down with measles (which, given the medical knowledge of the time, could be quite deadly). Pillsbury died of typhoid fever a few months later.[8]

In all, more soldiers died during the Civil War from the ravages of disease than from wounds received in battle. The same was true of Pierce's company and the 14th Regiment in general. A total of 125 men served in Company I of the 14th New Hampshire during the Civil War; 29 of them died. Of these, only five died in battle, while 24 died of disease. In the 14th Regiment as a whole, 1,260 men served during the war. 392 of them—31% of the regiment—died or were wounded or captured. This was much in keeping with other units during the war; in general, 30% of all the soldiers who enlisted into the service became casualties (killed, wounded, or captured)—the highest casualty rate of any war involving Americans. 221 of the 392 casualties were deaths. However, only 65 of the 221 deaths (a mere 5% of the total regiment) occurred in battle, while 156 men, or one in every eight soldiers who served in the regiment in the war, died of disease.[9]

Though he survived the war, Franklin Pierce did not escape affliction from its diseases. Though he rarely mentions even not feeling well in his diary, shortly after arriving in Poolesville, Pierce was stricken with an illness. He later termed it "chronic diarrhea" in his pension claims which he filed after the war. He received medicine for it during the war, but never spent time in the hospital. Whatever exactly it was at the start, it afflicted him for the rest of his life, causing stoppage and acute pain in his bowels.[10]

Life at Poolesville for the regiment soon settled into a dull daily regimen of chores, drill, and guard duty, marked by occasional forays against guerilla forces. Inspections were monthly, according to Pierce's diary (entry for 30 March). Drill was a common feature of camp life, especially when weather permitted it. Its purpose was to discipline the regiment into an effective fighting force, both as to its maneuverability on the battlefield as well as massing firepower. Pierce's diary entries record drills at various levels of the regiment's organization.

Tuesday, 13 January
A pleasant day, Out on battalion
drill for the first time in 3 weeks.

****

Monday, 19 January
A pleasant day. In camp all day. Battalion
drill fore and afternoon.

****

Monday, 2 February
A clear cold day.... Out on Company drill
afternoon for the first time in two weeks.

****

18

Saturday, 7 February
A fine day but very muddy walking... Two
company drills today.

****

Friday, 27 March
A very pleasant day.... Battalion drill.
Had some plank katridges. [blank cartridges,
for mock fire]

Guard duty was also a common assignment. In camp, soldiers were assigned picket duty guarding the perimeter of the camp, or headquarters, or, as mentioned earlier, prisoners. Usually dull, this duty sometimes was outright unpleasant, as one entry records:

Friday, 9 January
Like to have froze to death last night, no
tents for guard to sleep in at Headquarters.
Relieved at 9 1/2.

An important guard duty assignment was the local ferries, especially Conrad's Ferry (now White Ferry), just five miles to the west. With the Potomac River only a few miles away, Union troops guarded the ferries against any sneak attack by Confederate forces just over the other side:

Monday, 26 January
Left camp at 9 for picket duty on Conrads
Ferry Road.

****

Thursday, 5 March
A pleasant day but clouds up toward night. On
picket snowing and hailing at 9 p.m.
Countersign Rhodillen [Rhode Island] Lieut.
Adams of guard. Went to station on conrads
ferry road.

Drill, guard duty, inspections, scouting and skirmishing with the enemy not withstanding, life at Poolesville—at least, as Pierce's diaries report—was basically boring. A frequent, standard entry of Franklin's was simply, "In camp all day at Poolesville doing nothing." Under these circumstances, far from home in

19

Two views of the modern version of "Conrad's Ferry," now "White's Ferry": above, looking across to Virginia; below, looking back to the Maryland side. This ferry on the Potomac was a frequent guard duty assignment for soldiers of the 14th New Hampshire.

uncomfortable shelters, exposed to the elements and disease, with little to eat and that of poor quality, many soldiers simply quit. Desertion was a continual problem, as Pierce's diary reflects:

> **12 January**
> A pleasant day. Fateague duty today. Went
> down on the Conrads Ferry road to take down a
> stable with Lieut Chandler and fifty men.
> Five men deserted last night.

Those who stayed passed time by a variety of means. In one entry Pierce records spending time whittling a toy for his daughter Eva. Card playing was one of the most popular, from high-stakes poker games to simpler amusements. Pierce's preferences tended to the latter, no doubt due to his sense of responsibility to his family:

> **Wednesday, 28 January**
> Snowing all day but melts as fast as it
> comes.... In our quarters all day doing nothing
> but playing euchre and seven up.

Rumors about the conduct and course of the war were rife through the camp. One reached the 14th's camp in late January:

> **24 January**
> A pleasant day and quite warm. Got a letter
> from Hattie. Went over to town on the
> afternoon. Some signs of rain toward night.
> A rumor that Burnside had taken Lee or
> Longstreet and their divisions is going the
> rounds.

Pierce and his comrades might have wished it were so, but the rumor was sadly in error. The event to which it refers has been referred to in history books as General Ambrose Burnside's "Mud March." Seeking to atone for his disastrous defeat by Lee's forces at Fredericksburg in December, Burnside embarked in mid- winter on a flanking movement to trap Lee in Fredericksburg. The march had no sooner gotten under way when torrential rains hit, turning everything into mud that bogged down Union forces. Across the Rappahannock, the faces of the Confederate forces lit up in laughter. In Washington, the nation's leaders were red-faced in anger and embarrassment at yet another blundering effort by the Army of the Potomac. Burnside was sacked, replaced by General "Fighting Joe" Hooker. Hooker would receive high marks for improving morale and discipline in the army, but against Lee he fared no better than did his predecessors.

Pay-day, of course, was a major event in camp, particularly since it was never regular. Pierce records one payday on Wednesday, 7 January, and another on 28 February. Whether his pay came every month's end is not clear, but it seems never to have been dependable.

As winter gave way to spring and the weather warmed, the soldiers were able to pass time "playing ball," as Pierce enters in his diary on March 27. This was baseball, a game which had its origins in colonial New England and before that in eastern England, from which the New England colonists came.[11] The Civil War contributed more to the growth of baseball as the national pastime than any event before or since. Northern troops played it regularly. When prisoners of war, they taught the game to their Southern captors, who soon became avid fans of the sport.

Letter-writing and receiving was Franklin Pierce's favored way of spending his free time. Everyone in camp looked forward to the postmaster. Sometimes the mail carried care packages from home; Pierce records (18 January) his sergeant, Ransom Huntoon, getting a package in the mail that contained "some good things to eat." His wife Hattie, of course, was his most regular correspondent, but others back home in Bradford—His brother-in-law Len Jamieson, Len Spaulding, George Peaslee, et. al.—were also frequent pen-pals. Letters were a touch of home in a foreign, barren land, and eagerly looked forward to. One can sense Pierce's sadness in his diary entries when he did not receive an expected letter:

Tuesday, 3 February
A cold day. In camp all day. Mail today but
no letter for me. Wind blowing hard all day.

****

Wednesday, 4 February
A cold raw day. Went into the woods and
choped wood all day... No letter from home
for me.

Franklin and Hattie kept up a weekly exchange of letters during his time at Poolesville. One letter—March 10—contained a daguerreotype photo of him. Unfortunately, all of these letters were discarded or lost in the course of time.

The spring thaw brought with it a change in the regiment's circumstances. Pierce reports it in his entry for 2 April:

Thursday, 2 April
A pleasant day but some signs of a storm.
Right wing recd orders to march in the
morning. Wrote to Hattie.

The next day brought more changes:

Friday, 3 April

A pleasant day. Struck our tents and bid
farewell to Poolsville at 10 o.c. Co. B & D
stopped at Senaca. A & C at muddy branch and
Co. I at Great Falls. Arrived there at 8 1/2.
Slept on the boat.

Groups of men, Pierce among them, were detailed back to Poolesville over the
next several days to pick up lumber and materials left behind, but by the 7th the
regiment was in a new home at Great Falls. There is a break in Pierce's diary then
until 21 May. What had happened during that time is that the 14th had been
assigned, along with its brigade, to duty in Washington itself. Here they would stay
for the next nine months. Their assignment was multi-faceted, including patrol
duty, staff and headquarters assignments, continued drill, and even secret service
assignments. Chiefly, however, the 14th participated in guard duty at the Old
Capitol Prison.

Old Capitol Prison, located at First and "A" Streets, had a long and storied past
by the outbreak of the Civil War. Congress used it as a temporary legislature
following the torching of Washington by the British in the War of 1812. Afterwards
it served as a boarding house for many years, but by the advent of the war it was a

*A wartime view of Old Capitol Prison, located where the Supreme Court building
stands today, across from the modern Capitol building.*

dilapidated, derelict building infested with lice and rodents. The army converted it into a prison for Confederate soldiers, spies, Federal political prisoners, even contraband slaves needing shelter until they could find work. In place of iron bars, the prison windows were boarded by wood slats. Life inside the prison was relaxed, even pleasant compared to the more infamous Civil War prisons such as Andersonville, Elmira, Libby, and Florence. The men passed the time playing poker and "muggins," a form of dominoes. Whiskey was plentiful and easily obtained. The food, if poor in quality, was adequate. The Confederate POW's even received dietary supplements in the form of food gifts from rebel sympathizers in Washington.[12]

Security at the prison depended, not on the building itself, but the detachments of soldiers assigned guard duty. Franklin Pierce received his share of assignments; apparently regarding them with scorn as beneath his rank of corporal:

Tuesday, 2 June
Doing guard duty over at Old Capital prison as
a private....

Despite being in the nation's capital, life in the summer of 1863 was, from Pierce's diary entries, dull and routine. He writes of being lonely, and his illness contracted back in Poolesville sidelined him more than once. In addition, there were worries from the homefront: His first-born child, daughter Eva, was ill. Then on 20 October came the terrible news. Pierce's one-line entry in his diary starkly recorded his shock and despair:

Tuesday, 20 October
Little Eva died.

Pierce applied for and was granted a two-week furlough to go home to his family. He left by train on Thursday the 29th in the evening, arrived in New York City the next day, leaving the following evening, and arrived in Clairmont, New Hampshire late that night. Staying overnight with someone he knew, he got to Bradford by stage at 8:00 pm. One hour later, he recorded:

Saturday, 31 October
Arrived at B. at eight and got down home about
nine. Poor little Hattie was sitting by the
window when she saw me. Glad to see me god
bless her.

Pierce spent the next twelve days at home, attending to family business. Perhaps for the need of cash, or the inability of Hattie to maintain everything on their farm, Pierce mentions in his 5 November entry selling the family's steers to a neighbor for 70 dollars.

"Little Eva" Pierce, who died of diphtheria in 1863. Holding her is Lucetta Pierce, Cummings Pierce's daughter.

The time at home, though welcome, ended all too soon, and Franklin's fortnight leave came to a close. Franklin had been fortunate in the war thus far; his duty had been relatively risk-free. But the prospect of returning to a war that seemed to have no end in sight, with total uncertainty about where his unit would be assigned, was almost too much for everyone to bear. On his return to Washington he wrote:

Thursday, 12 November
Started for Washington. Left Hattie and all
the rest crying, and I feel as tho I had left
all I hold dear on Earth behind and I have.
May we all need to part no more soon. God
bless my wife and children.

Pierce arrived back with his unit two days later. Though back on duty, his heart, of course, was still with his family. His spirits were buoyed by news that "All well at home" (21 November), but there were also days of depression, or "the blues" as he called them (26 November) as he continued to grieve for his lost daughter and situation in general. The diary records, unlike past entries, more frequent postings of money back home to assist the family. Undoubtedly Hattie's work at home was unable to provide enough for the family to live on without help from Franklin sending more of his pay home. He even pawned unneeded clothes to obtain money to send home. Life on assignment in Washington remained, however, basically routine and unchanged as the third winter of the war wore on. Pierce's diary entries stop with a short note on the weather 3 December. No doubt he started another and continued writing during 1864, but—for reasons which shall be explained further on—the 1864 diary was lost. That was not just his family's loss, but posterity's as well. The year to come would bring a series of adventures as Pierce and his Granite State comrades saw service on several fronts of the war, culminating in a magnificent campaign with General Phil Sheridan. For Franklin, it would also mean a brush with death the following Fall.

CHAPTER THREE

Prelude to the Final Campaign

By February 1864 Benjamin Franklin Pierce had served a year and a half in the Union army without, aside from a few skirmishes with rebel guerilla units, having known the heat of battle. His duty had been confined to the nation's capital and vicinity, manning the defenses of the city and guarding prisoners at Old Capitol Prison. The regiment was quite skilled in drill and maneuvers, but had no real combat experience. Officially the 14th New Hampshire belonged to the XXII Corps, Military District of Washington of the Department of Washington, commanded by Major General Christopher Auger.[1] Franklin Pierce was now a sergeant, having been promoted on the 26th of January.[2]

Beginning in February, however, life changed drastically for the men of the 14th New Hampshire. Over the next year the Granite State men would see action on nearly every front of the war: From the defenses of Washington to Louisiana, back to the siege of Petersburg in Virginia, to the campaign with Sheridan in the Shenandoah Valley, and finally to Sherman's march through the Carolinas.

A few days after Franklin's promotion, General Henry "Old Brains" Halleck, General-in-Chief of the war effort, ordered the 14th New Hampshire to proceed to Harpers Ferry "ready for immediate service in the field."[3] Their purpose was to assist forces there in repelling attacks by Confederate guerilla units. Most likely these were forces under the command of John Moseby, a guerilla leader whose efforts were so effective that Loudoun County in northern Virginia was known as "Moseby's Confederacy" for much of the war. The 14th arrived and became part of the Third Brigade, Third Division, Sixth Army Corps, but again saw little combat action; what they did do was nearly freeze to death in their shelter-tents in the mountains which rise above the historic river town of Harpers Ferry that had already seen more than enough fighting during the war.

By the end of the month Moseby's threat had diminished, and the 14th was called back to Washington, arriving on the 25th. Cheering news greeted them upon their arrival from their frigid experience: The regiment was granted a two-week furlough home to vote in elections before their next assignment: Louisiana.

Leaving Washington, the regiment arrived in Concord on the 28th. The soldiers departed to their home towns for their fortnight's break from the war and joyful reunions with their loved ones. Hattie's 1864 diary records his arrival on the first day of March:

March 1, 1864
Pleasant day and a verry happy day for me.
Frank came home. Mr. Cheney came in the
evening.

Two wartime views of Harpers Ferry. The 14th New Hampshire passed through here in February of 1864.

Franklin spent his leave visiting with friends and neighbors. A rainy day March 6 cancelled plans for a Sunday buggy ride and confined Franklin and Hattie inside their house, "courting" all day long, according to Hattie's cryptic comment in her diary.

Franklin's pleasure at being home was lessened by a battle with diphtheria. In retrospect he was lucky: Had he been forced to fight the disease in the field, during the raw, damp months of March and April, it might have killed him. Such had been the unhappy lot of quite a few members of the 14th regiment during their duty in and about Washington. As it was, Franklin could recuperate in the comforts of home.

His illness also extended his leave: When the regiment left New Hampshire for Louisiana on the 16th, Franklin stayed behind. Hattie writes in her diary on the 17th, "The reg [regiment] has gone." Franklin remained at home, recuperating; Hattie writes on the 21st, "Dear Frank is here with me and I am happy." But a few days later the inevitable came:

March 23
Pleasant day but oh my dear Frank has got to
go off. He went to the village to see the
doctor today....

Then, two days later, came the sad parting:

Mar. 25
Beautiful day. We Frank and I went to Concord
and it has been one of the saddest days of my life.
I had to part with my dearest husban.
Oh God bless and protect him shall be my
earnest prayer.

****

Mar. 26
Another pleasant day but I miss my dear Frank
so I get so lonely I can't stay here nothing.
Evening find me at home but oh it is so lonely
I miss the well known home.

With his departure came the continual, anxious question every parent asks of their son, every lover of her beloved, every spouse of her husband in time of war: "Where is he?"

Mar. 27
Pleasant day but oh such a lonely one to me.
Frances has been here today and Cynth. Oh if
I only knew where my dear Frank was.

Frank was on his way to join his unit, now in transit to Louisiana. Leaving New Hampshire on the 16th, the regiment arrived in New York City and set sail from there on the 20th. The trip was by no means serene: Off Cape Hattaras their ship encountered a terrible storm. The regimental historian later remarked about it:

> ...a long ocean voyage, with a hurricane off Hattaras, and forebodings of foundering so realistic as to stir feelings of horror in the writer thirty years after. The battered, crowded, transport crawled into Hilton Head, and the Fourteenth camped in deep sand and shelter-tents, under glorious palm trees and pitiless rain clouds.[4]

Through storm and peril on the sea, the regiment finally reached its destination, arriving at the end of March. When Franklin rejoined his comrades is not certain. Along the way he penned a short letter to his daughter, Bertha Frances, his only letter to survive the war. Though undated, it bears all the marks of a man who has just left home, facing an uncertain future in a war, and who longs to be back home in the security of his family:

Darling little daughter:

> Mama says I must write a letter to you and so I will do so and put it in her letter. And now what shall I say to you? Has little Frankie been a good girl since Papa left home? I hope she has for I shall bring her a new dollie when I come, and I should feel bad if I have to give it to a naughty little girl and she must kiss Mama for Papa and when she says her prayers at night at mama's knee she must remember to pray for Papa and must write a little letter to me. Good night my little darling. Papa would give anything if he could see you tonight.

> Papa

Following their arrival in Louisiana, the men from the Granite State were assigned to duty in the defenses of New Orleans while the bulk of Union forces in the region were engaged in General Nathaniel Banks' "Red River Campaign" through northwestern Louisiana.

The Red River Campaign evolved out of newly-appointed General-in-Chief Ulysses Grant's strategy of a coordinated Union offensive to pressure the Confederacy's thin resources in hopes of achieving a breakthrough wherever possible. Grant sought to set Union armies into motion on all fronts: Meade attacking Lee in Virginia, Sherman moving on Atlanta, Sigel in the Shenandoah, Butler along the Virginia Peninsula, Banks in Louisiana by moving on Mobile, Alabama. But bureaucratic interference diverted Banks from his march on Mobile to send him up the Red River through northwestern Louisiana to seize cotton and extend Union control west through Louisiana and into east Texas.

Setting off from Alexandria on March 15, Banks' force of 20,000 men consisted of a division of the Nineteenth Corps (to which the 14th would be assigned a few months later) and two divisions from the Thirteenth Corps. Opposing him were

Bertha Frances Pierce, about the age when her father wrote her the above letter.

over 9,000 Confederates under the command of General Richard Taylor, son of the late President. Banks' army moved up the Red River with initial success against little opposition. Shreveport, 120 miles northwest, was his goal. Concurrently, a second Union force began to move south from Arkansas, thus forming with Banks' army a pincer movement on the rebel forces. By the first week in April, Banks had covered half the distance to his goal of Shreveport.

But from there everything went downhill. His march from Natchitoches beginning April 6 bogged down in the sparsely-settled wilderness of northwestern

Louisiana. Also, the second-half of the pincer movement, the Union force in Arkansas, was turned back in its efforts to link up with Banks. Two days later Banks' force ran up against Taylor's well-positioned force, now swelled to almost 15,000 soldiers, at a place called Sabine's Crossroads. Taylor's force dealt the Union troops a decisive defeat, which spelled the end of the Red River offensive and began a tortuous retreat back towards New Orleans that finally and mercifully ended in late May. Exhausted, the army never did move on Mobile, as Grant had intended them to do.

During this offensive the 14th New Hampshire was shifted about various defenses in and about New Orleans, serving duty at Camp Parapet, Carrollton, Jefferson City, and on Lake Pontchartrain. The hot, muggy weather of Louisiana and its insect-laden swamps brought disease and death to quite a number of soldiers, unaccustomed as they were to Louisiana's strange climate in comparison to that of their native state.[5]

On June 7th the 14th received orders to move up the Mississippi and join Banks' army in Morganzia. There the regiment was assigned to the First Brigade of the Second Division, Nineteenth Corps, commanded by General William Emory. General Cuvier Grover commanded the division and General Henry Birge commanded the brigade. For the remainder of the war the 14th New Hampshire would travel and fight under the colors of the XIX Corps. The end of the Red River campaign freed the XIX Corps for duty elsewhere. As Grant's spring offensive against Robert E. Lee settled into trench warfare around Petersburg and Richmond, extra units were needed to fill in the lines. Early in July, the Corps was returned north to join the fighting on the eastern front. The regiment set sail from New

The camp of the 14th New Hampshire while at Morganzia, Louisiana, during the Red River Campaign.

32

Orleans in two groups: One—Companies E, F, G, and K—under Major Gardiner; the other, under Colonel Wilson, comprised of Companies A, B, C, D, H, and I (Pierce's).[6]

During their voyage, Lee cut loose a small army from his main force pinned down in Petersburg and Richmond. Jubal Early and his force was sent to the North through the Shenandoah Valley. Early achieved greater success than expected; he very nearly marched right up Pennsylvania Avenue to the White House. First sweeping the Shenandoah clear of Federal troops, he then proceeded to use the valley as a channel to threaten Maryland and the capital. By mid-July he was within sight of the dome on the Capitol building. The North was panic stricken.

Arriving at Fortress Monroe on the Virginia Peninsula, Major Gardiner's wing of the regiment was sent in haste to join other units Grant was moving from the Petersburg front to the defence of Washington. They arrived just in time to bolster the Washington lines and convince Early and his rebels to turn back.

Meanwhile, Wilson's wing, along with the 75th New York Infantry regiment, was detailed out to join the Army of the Potomac at Bermuda Hundred. Arriving there on July 21st, the troops saw some action as part of General Hancock's II Corps' diversionary attack at Deep Bottom during the Battle of the Crater. They suffered a few casualties, merely a taste of things to come.[7]

With Early's assault on Washington turned aside and the botched Battle of the Crater over, both wings of the regiment were again reunited with the Nineteenth Corps near Winchester, Virginia, in mid-August as part of the newly-formed Army of the Shenandoah, Major General Philip Sheridan commanding. The men of the 14th New Hampshire were about to participate in one of the decisive campaigns of the Civil War, under one of its greatest generals.

CHAPTER FOUR

On The Homefront

The fourth summer of the war wore on, with no end in sight. Speculation abounded that Lincoln would not be re-elected. In northern Virginia, Franklin Pierce prepared for what would be his heaviest fighting of the war.

Back home in Bradford, New Hampshire, Hattie Pierce struggled to endure the hardships the war placed on her and their children. It was a lonely struggle; at one point in her 1864 diary (August 13) Hattie described her lot with a sigh, "Oh dear how lonely it is to be a grass widow and I must go to bed alone." In the parlance of the day a "grass widow" was a divorced or separated woman. A woman who had just lost her husband wore clothing that people called "widow's weeds"; hence the term for a woman separated or divorced from her husband "grass widow."

Hattie's was not an exceptional case; many wives had seen their husbands march off to war, leaving them behind as "grass widows." What was life like for those left behind at home by the war? The terse lines of Hattie's 1864 diary give a picture of the daily lot of the Civil War wife: Her loneliness, her anxious longing for her beloved one off in battle, her daily struggle just to survive, and the ways she found comfort and a little peace and joy amid the struggle.

When Franklin returned to Bradford with his new bride, the couple took up residence with his parents on the family farm. The Pierce clan lived a few miles south of Bradford above what is now named Lake Massasecum, but then, Bradford Pond. An 1858 map of Bradford reveals a typical, self-contained New England town of just over a thousand inhabitants clustered in smaller neighborhoods known as "Bradford Mills," "Bradford Center," and "Bradford Corner." Outlying the town were scattered farms, such as the Pierce's. The railroad, Franklin's source of employment, ran just north of the town (present day Route 103) to its end-of-the-line depot in Bradford.[1]

The Pierce lands were shared by Nathan, Jr. and his brother, Cummings. Driving along present-day highway 114, one turns right just after reaching the north end of Lake Massasecum onto what is now "Breezy Hill Road." Crossing a bridge over a small creek, the road forks. Breezy Hill continues on the left, towards Bradford; a few hundred yards further was the home Nathan Pierce, Jr. built. The right fork (now "Old Pierce Road") goes a few hundred yards up Guiles' Hill to two homes: The larger one is the home of Cummings Pierce; the smaller one is the original family home, built by Nathan Pierce, Sr.

Cummings Pierce was a farmer and also served several years as one of the town's "selectmen" (a councilman). A contemporary description characterized him as "...one of the earliest risers and most industrious and frugal of farmers, and consequently he has been very successful and prosperous."[2] His prosperity was due, apparently, to a no-nonsense approach to work, witnessed by another

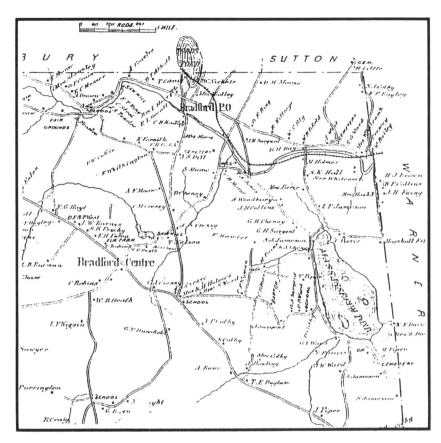

An 1858 map, showing the town of Bradford, the lake, and outlying farms. The Pierce lands can be found just above the northwest tip of Massasecum Pond.

contemporary story about him. A custom of the day was to give the field hands rum as they harvested the crops. Cummings was the first in the town to substitute hot coffee instead.[3]

Just off the road to Cummings' house, atop a hill, was the Pierce family cemetery. Then commanding a clear view of the lake, today trees obscure the view from the cemetery. Stone slabs mark the graves of Cummings Pierce, his wife Caroline, Nathan and Phoebe Pierce, and daughters Susan (Collins) and Mary (who never married). The lake area, still a scenic beauty, has become a summer vacation and retirement area populated by small homes and cabins.

Franklin's father, Nathan Pierce, Jr., was 70 years old when his son went off to war; his mother, Abigail, was 64. Hattie and Franklin's move back to Bradford had been occasioned, most likely, by the advanced years of his parents. So, when Franklin joined the military, Hattie found herself trying to care, not only for her two young daughters, but for her in-laws as well. It was not an ideal arrangement by any means, even if it did provide Hattie and the children with food and shelter. Descendants in later generations recalled the shock of how the fun-loving Hattie, far from her own family and native culture, had to adjust to the staid, structured life of a small, isolated New England town in the home of her strait-laced in-laws.

Nevertheless, Hattie adjusted to her new life and established relationships with the people of the town and her family. The same 1858 map bears the names of many of the people mentioned by Hattie in her diary as her circle of friends, relatives, and acquaintances: Aunt Caroline, Len and Cynthia Jameson (Frank's younger sister), Len Spaulding, Dr. Cheney, George Sargent, Wheeler, Hall, Fritsch, Cressy, and others.[4] These people formed the tapestry of her social life. These and others were the people she met on a daily basis, for business, for the pleasure of a visit, to share a meal with. In today's nation of strangers, where people form and break relationships constantly, such a life is foreign to many. People today resort to therapists, support groups, and the like to find solace for their problems and loneliness. But in a small, rural town such as 19th-century Bradford, the people that made up one's life were not just passing acquaintances, but a firm means of support that enabled people to bear the struggles of life.

And life was a struggle. Lacking any of our modern conveniences, daily life was an unending series of chores and tasks that had to be done, simply to survive. It took a hardy breed of person to carve out a life in the wilderness of the New Hampshire hills, especially in winter when, as Hattie used to say, the weather turned "as cold as Greenland." The lakes began to freeze over in November and the snows and cold limited outside activity. Life for Hattie, her family, and friends was a matter of the essentials: shelter, food, and clothing.

Fortunately for Hattie, providing shelter was not a problem, living as she did with her husband's relations. Providing food was not a problem either, because from the family farm came an ample supply of vegetables: Peas, turnips, cabbage, squash, beets. Beans were a regular staple of their diet. Later generations recalled how every Saturday night Hattie made Boston baked beans for supper. The practice was as old as Puritan New England: Forbidden to work on the Sabbath, families cooked a sufficient quantity of beans or peas on Saturday to provide food for Sunday (hence the name "Beantown" for Boston). Known as "pease porridge," the dish was so common that it gave rise to the familiar nursery rhyme of children:

> "Pease porridge hot,
> Pease porridge cold,
> Pease porridge in the pot,
> Nine days old."[5]

In other aspects Hattie's diary reveals cooking and dietary patterns typical of New England; ways that predominate in the family to this day: Baked or boiled dishes, pies, cookies, fruits, tea. The meals were simple and basic. A dinner might simply consist of flapjacks, as Hattie recorded one evening, beans, or fruit. Pies, such as pumpkin and apple, were made in large quantities and kept on shelves in a cold cellar for later eating (New Englanders also favored mince meat pies, as a way of preserving meat). A favorite summer and spring activity was to go "a-berrying." Hattie writes of going "a-berrying" for strawberries in June and blackberries in August to make jelly. One September day she notes discoloring her hands so much she was frustrated at not being able to sew. Fall brought apple harvest time; she writes in October of being weary from "climbing trees and gathering apples." Today traces of the berry bushes and apple orchards originally planted by the Pierces still can be found amid the woods on the hills of their old homestead.

Slaughtering a hog or cow was an important event that provided the main source of meat for the family. Occasionally a neighbor would stop by with a gift of food; Hattie writes (January 24, 1864), "George Spaulding brought over a mess of fish." And if there was someone in need, hospitality dictated that food be shared. Hattie recalls one incident (February 24) of "some old straglers [stragglers] came in and wanted some breakfast. We gave them some."

Hattie herself, like many women of the time, supplied the family's clothing. Sewing was not only a necessary skill in life; for Hattie it was a family tradition and mini-business. Hattie learned to sew from her mother, Hannah Goodwin, who was quite a seamstress in her own right, according to the family's oral tradition. Hattie sewed all her family clothing, as well as earning herself some money during the war sewing, as she termed them in her diary, "drawers"—women's undergarments. A typical entry in her diary might note the following among the day's achievements:

> ### January 20
> Wednesday. Quite cold and windy. I have been
> to the corner. I got 15 pairs of drawers
> today. There had been no one here today. I
> expect to get a letter from Frank.

The "corner" was that part of Bradford known as Bradford Corner. This area, now the present junction of Route 114, Main Street, and Old Warner Road, has long been a site of businesses in Bradford. One of the buildings there even acquired the name of "Petticoat Lane" and was a dress shop.[6] Hattie would make her drawers, take them down to "The Corners," and sell them to a business there. With the money she received, Hattie would travel down Main Street further to "Carr's Store" (mentioned occasionally in her diary) and buy the staples she needed for her home, plus more supplies for her work. Nearby Carr's Store was the old post office, too, at which Hattie often waited anxiously for a letter from her husband. Her little business was a scandal to her straitlaced mother and aunt-in-laws, who regarded the making of women's underwear as a less-than-savory occupation, however

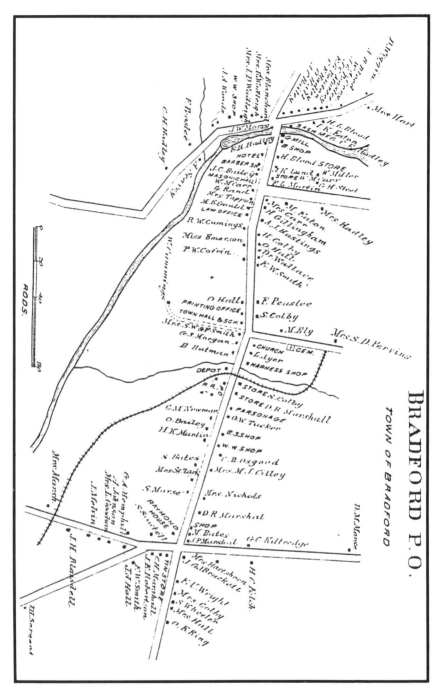

A map of the town of Bradford, in 1858, identifying public buildings and residences.

Lake Massasecum (formerly called Massasecum Pond), looking towards Guiles' Hill and the Pierce lands. Below is the bridge over which one crosses to the roads leading to the Pierce homes.

The Cummings Pierce house (above); the Pierce family cemetery atop Guiles' Hill (below).

Two views of the house built by Nathan Pierce, Sr.: above, in 1931, and below, today. The house stands just behind the Cummings Pierce home.

Two views of Nathan Pierce, Jr.'s home, occupied by Franklin and Hattie Pierce during the war and later by Cynthia and Len Jameson: above, in 1931, below, today.

Above: Bradford Corners, as one enters Bradford today. Below: the center of Bradford town, where the rail line used to end. The depot used to stand just off to the right of the photo.

Two places oft-frequented by Hattie Pierce: Carr's Store (above) and, to the left of Carr's Store, just down Main Street, the former site of the post office (below).

necessary. But the business did enable Hattie to earn some money which, in addition to what Franklin sent home, helped her get through the war.

The diary entry just cited, brief as it is, is a microcosm of Hattie's life on the homefront. Besides the reference to the arduous New Hampshire winter, her business activity and various associations in town, the entry also reveals an important aspect of Hattie's social life: visits from the neighbors, and letters to Frank.

This was an age, one must remember, that knew nothing of our society's craving for entertainment. People did not find their entertainment in things, but in each other's company. Visiting, or going to dinner, was an important part of life. Hattie's diary is filled with entries about who visited her each day, and records the lonely days when she saw no one. Visits were an important ritual; they provided an opportunity for the sharing of common joys and sorrows, the news of the town or the war (including, surely, not a little gossip), and seeking advice and counsel on dealing with problems that arose in life. Apparently, most visits were unannounced. People would decide to visit someone, wander over to their house, and walk on in. Sometimes this produced unexpected and awkward surprises, as Hattie records in one such instance:

August (date illegible)
I washed and laid down to rest my weery bones
and did not chang my dress until I was caught
Dr. Cheny came in and I skadded [skedaddled]
upstairs to change my apparel. I was
mortified for there was my legs plane to be seen....

Hattie also found release from the tedium of daily life (and the restrictions of life in a small town) by travels to visit friends and relatives. Her diaries frequently record trips to visit friends in Concord. Hattie also had relatives in Vermont, and in late spring and much of the summer of 1864 she visited her side of the family there.

Church was another important element in the rhythm of life in Civil War Bradford. It occupied a much more central place in the town's life than today; serving not only as the means to nourish faith, but also as a place for people to gather, socialize, and bear each other's burdens. Often people attended several services in one day. It is interesting to find, too, that some of the problems a mother with two small children had in church over a hundred years ago were not all that unlike ones parents have today:

July 3
Oh dear what a lone some day. I went to
church this morning but Frankie was so naughty
I could not stay. Went again this afternoon.

The other important aspect mentioned in Hattie's January 19 diary entry is her anticipation of receiving a letter from her husband. Letter writing, a lost art today, was also a significant activity of people's lives in the Civil War era. It was the only way people could keep in touch over long distances; it helped fill up the day and ward off boredom and loneliness. Most of all for Hattie, it was a welcome relief to know that, at least by the date of his letter, her Frank was still alive and well.

An occasional sad event was the funeral of a soldier returned home from the front. It was a reminder to Hattie of her own soldier-husband's precarious situation. Her attempt to make sense of the tragedy of death is similar to that of Lincoln's remark in his second inaugural address, that God had his own purposes, inscrutable to humans:

Sept. 4
Father [Nathan Pierce, Jr.] and I went to the
firnel of Mr. Newton Cheeny [Cheney] Poor
soldier was not permitted to see Friends and
home but Gods way is not our way It rains
slowly to night enuf to give any one the blues.

Another common activity of the time was attending political meetings to hear speakers extol the war effort or campaign for office. Hattie records going to one when Franklin was home on the 5th of March; she also mentions several others—particularly when a speaker was especially good (such as "the soul stirring speech by the honorable Mr. Potters" on October 25.) The center of political life in New England was the town meeting, at which the important issues, be they local or national, were debated.

These town meetings reveal a time far more sophisticated and advanced in its political dialogue than our "modern" age. Our era finds it almost impossible to engage in intelligent political debate; important issues are reduced to slick slogans that fit into fifteen-second "sound bytes." The Civil War era, absent of today's technology, placed greater importance on the ability of speakers to convince their audiences by argument and debate. The famous Lincoln-Douglass debates, for example, sometimes lasted up to six hours. More amazing, though, is that people remained and listened to political debates and speeches for as long as they lasted. It was an age in which the spoken word and reasoned argument dominated, unlike our era's captivity to televised or printed images that seek to promote, not reasoned thought and decisions, but immediate, unreflective responses.

Daily house chores, her little business, rounds of visits, church, political meetings: so passed Hattie's days on the homefront in 1864. Life for most every person is a day in, day out stream of tedious chores and insignificant events taken for granted, but Hattie's days were burdened by two greater longings. One was for her lost daughter, "little Eva," who had died the autumn before. Hattie continued to mourn her loss, and now and then her grief surfaces in a diary entry. For example,

Anna Mae Pierce, the eldest surviving daughter, as a schoolgirl.

the anniversary of Eva's birth was a painful reminder of her absence:

Aug. 9
Well another day is gone. The birthday of my
lost Eva my precious angel. I little thought
on her last birthday that it would be the
last. Oh my Eva little Eva.

But most of all, Hattie pined deeply for her husband who was away at war. Hattie's entries record a roller-coaster of her emotions as she longed to hear from Frank. They reveal her anxiety when a letter did not come, her rejoicing when a letter arrived, and the never-ending hope that the war would end soon and Frank would come home. Her sparse lines vividly reveal the warmth and tenderness of her love for Frank.

The summer of 1864 found Hattie visiting her relatives in Vermont. Bertha Frances, their youngest daughter, accompanied her; the elder, Anna Mae, evidently stayed home with her grandparents (strangely, Anna Mae is mentioned little in the dairies). When she returned to Bradford in August, little could Hattie have realized that the war would soon be over for Frank. Although it would last several more months for the rest of the nation, Frank's last involvement would be in one of the great and decisive campaigns of the war: Sheridan in the Shenandoah.

47

CHAPTER FIVE

The Final Campaign

Most of the first two years of his life in the Union Army were, by and large, uneventful for Benjamin Franklin Pierce. Other than traveling over a large part of the United States, his duty had been mostly restricted to behind-the-front defenses and prison duty. Beginning in August 1864, however, all that would quickly change for Pierce and his comrades in arms. They were about to participate in one of the major, decisive campaigns of the war. In the next two months, Pierce would see more combat action than in all his previous time in the army. It included a near brush with death that would end his active army life and scar him for the rest of his days.

The end of July found General Ulysses Grant, commander of the Union armies, in a serious dilemma. His spring campaign of an all-front, coordinated offensive had unfolded poorly and failed to achieve the objectives he had wanted. His own immediate command, the Army of the Potomac, had incurred such massive losses that critics in the North were calling for his replacement. So strong was the criticism that Lincoln's re-election was highly doubtful.

But Grant had succeeded in doing what no other Union general had done in the two prior years of the war: Bottling up Lee in a siege. It deprived Lee of his greatest strength, the ability to maneuver against his opponents. Lee knew the danger before him; earlier that spring he had said to his subordinates, "We must destroy this army of Grant's before it gets to the James River. If he gets there it will become a siege, and then it will be a mere question of time."[1]

But Grant's army on the siege lines of Petersburg was exhausted from the non-stop fighting which had begun long ago in May; also, pinning Lee down in a siege restricted the Army of the Potomac's ability to maneuver, too. The result was a stalemate on the front lines, one that Lee now acted to take the offensive before the siege forced him to capitulate.

It was a move born of desperation. Grant had managed to lock Lee into a strangle-hold siege, and Lee knew it would only be a matter of time before he would be forced to submit. Sherman was moving on Atlanta. With a military victory growing dimmer and dimmer with each passing day, a way had to be found to win the war psychologically; that was, to do something which would weaken the North and its political leadership and break its will to fight and force a negotiated peace. With the national election approaching and Lincoln's re-election still up for grabs, Lee sought for a way to tip public sentiment toward the Democrats who wanted to sue for peace. It was worth a try; indeed, it was probably the South's last hope.

Lee cut General Jubal Early loose from the Petersburg front with an army of 15,000 men. His express orders: Remove any threat of Union control from the Shenandoah Valley, the vital food supply for Lee's army. The second: Do whatever

General Jubal Early

he could to create havoc in the Union rear, so as to force Grant to divert troops from Petersburg, or even abandon it altogether to protect his capital.

"Old Jube," as he was called, was an irascible cuss who cared little for social amenities. Though opposed to the Confederate secession, when war broke out he immediately joined the Confederate service as the commander of the 24th Virginia Infantry. At Antietam he was a brigade commander in Stonewall Jackson's Corps. In 1864 Lee raised him to the level of corps commander and sent him to campaign in the Shenandoah Valley.

Early succeeded admirably in pursuing the objectives Lee had set for him. Setting out in June, Early's small army made short work of Union forces in the Shenandoah Valley, then moved down the valley to wreak havoc in the third Confederate invasion of the North. Crossing the Potomac River on July 6, Early's forces retraced Lee's 1862 invasion route to Frederick, Maryland, then turned south to menace Washington. A delaying action by a hastily-organized Union army at Monocacy River south of Frederick July 9 caused Early's army to lose a day's march.

It was a vital loss: The intervening time allowed additional Union forces from the Petersburg front to rush to the defence of Washington. Two days later Early and his men came within five miles of the White House, within sight of the Capitol dome. On July 12 the armies skirmished along the northern out-skirts of the capital, with President Lincoln looking on (and nearly getting himself shot).

Early decided that Washington's defenses were too strong to risk attacking with his small army, and the city would be impossible to hold if he did manage to take it. Having put a scare into the entire city, Early retreated back into Virginia, marching through Poolesville (Franklin Pierce's camp of two years before), along the way. His military draw had been a huge psychological victory, adding momentum to the election-year opponents of Lincoln who sought a negotiated end to the weary war.

Though Washington was safe and Early was back in Virginia, things did not get any better for Union forces there. Later in July Early defeated another Union force at Kernstown, south of Winchester, and drove them back out of the valley. In addition to their military success, Early's forces succeeded in exacting tribute (in valued Northern greenbacks) from the Union towns they conquered: $200,000 from Frederick, and another $20,000 from Hagerstown, Maryland. When Chambersburg, Pennsylvania, refused to ante up $500,000 by July 30th, Early ordered the town burned.[2]

Grant had had enough. Cutting through the red tape of Washington bureaucracy, he demanded and received the authority to consolidate all Union forces in northern

Major General Philip Sheridan, commander of the Army of the Shenandoah in the fall of 1864. The inscription on the photo identifies it as after the Battle of Cedar Creek, though it actually may have been taken a few months before.

Brigadier General Cuvier Grover, commander of the XIX Corps.

Virginia into one command. This he gave to General Philip Sheridan, and entrusted him to put an end to Early's antics.

General "Little Phil" Sheridan was, in Grant's estimation, one of the ablest soldiers of the war. Only 33, Sheridan, like Grant, had been raised in Ohio and had graduated from West Point. Their association went back to the Battle of Shiloh in April 1862, when Sheridan was yet only a regimental commander. It was at the Battle of Missionary Ridge that Sheridan distinguished himself in Grant's eyes as Sheridan's men made an infantry charge up the mountainside that turned a stalemate into a major Union victory.

Small, bandy-legged, with piercing Mongol-like eyes, possessed of an acerbic tongue and quick Irish temper, Sheridan hardly looked the part of a general. But in battle he was bold, fearless, and an inspirational leader. He was hard-driving, yet fiercely loyal to those in his command. He cared deeply for the welfare of his troops, unwilling to waste lives in a battle where he was not sure of victory.

When Grant came east in March of 1864, he brought Sheridan with him shortly thereafter and made him commander of all the cavalry units in the Army of the Potomac. He had distinguished himself a few months earlier by his famous Raid on Richmond, which resulted in the death of the legendary Confederate cavalry commander J.E.B. Stuart at the Battle of Yellow Tavern May 11.

Now in August of 1864 Sheridan was elevated to the command of an entire army: the Army of the Shenandoah. It was comprised of the veteran VI Corps from the Army of the Potomac, the well-trained but untested XIX Corps, and a new corps, the VIII Corps, comprised of former units in the area of northern Virginia, and three divisions of cavalry—two from Sheridan's former command in the Army of the

Brigadier General Henry Birge, Franklin Pierce's brigade commander.

Potomac. Pierce's half of the 14th New Hampshire, fresh from its participation in the attack on Deep Bottom during the Battle of the Crater, linked up with the other half of the regiment to join the XIX Corps in mid-August. The 14th's place in the organization for the XIX Corps is shown in the following table:

Corps Commander:	BG William H. Emory
First Division:	BG James McMillan
Second Division:	BG Cuvier Grover
First Brigade:	BG Henry W. Birge
9th Connecticut	
12th Maine	
14th Maine	
26th Massachusetts	
14th New Hampshire	
75th New York	
Second Brigade:	Col. Edward Molineux
Third Brigade:	Col. Daniel McCauley
Fourth Brigade:	Col. David Shunk
Artillery Brigade:	Maj. Albert Bradbury[3]

Sheridan's orders from Grant were as clear and unequivocal as Lee's had been to Early two months before: Get rid of Early once and for all, and destroy the usefulness of the Shenandoah Valley as a source of supply for the Confederates.

From the start of the conflict the Shenandoah Valley was doomed to suffer the ravages of war. It was, as has been mentioned, a vital supply center for the Confederate armies. Bordered on the east and west by mountains, the valley provided a natural screen for any armies moving north and south through it on the macadamized Route 11. Confederate armies used the route several times throughout the war to launch attacks on the North, most recently the heretofore mentioned expeditions of General Early. The Valley's importance to the South was no better summarized than by the concise statement of Stonewall Jackson: "If the Valley is lost, Virginia is lost."[4]

Sheridan's task was to make sure the Valley was lost to the Confederacy, permanently. Grant's orders to Sheridan left no doubt about that:

> It is desirable that nothing should be left to invite the enemy to return. Take all provisions, forage, stock...such as cannot be consumed, destroy...If the war is to last another year, we want the Shenandoah Valley to remain a barren waste.[5]

Sheridan proceeded cautiously, however, in achieving his goals. Rather than risk another embarrassing defeat for the Union army, he husbanded his forces, bided his time, waiting for a time and place to his liking. He occupied Winchester, at the northernmost entrance to the Valley, but retreated before Early in mid-August. Sheridan took up positions on a line running from Harpers Ferry on the Potomac south to Berryville, some ten miles to the east of Winchester. During this period the XIX Corps, including the 14th New Hampshire, was involved in minor fights at Berryville September 3 and Lock's Ford September 13.

A sketch of the camp of the 14th New Hampshire Infantry near Berryville, Virginia, in September 1864.

Both sides miscalculated the other's total troop strength; Sheridan overestimating Early's, Lee underestimating Sheridan's. Lee's miscalculation would prove fatal to Early's cause. In early September Lee, needing all possible troops on the Petersburg front, recalled a division of Early's army to his own. Sheridan soon learned of the move. Through the link of a black man who went into Winchester weekly to sell vegetables, Sheridan obtained information about the activities of Early's army from Rebecca Wright, a Quaker school teacher in Winchester sympathetic to the Union cause. Learning of Early's reduced strength, Sheridan resolved that it was time to act. The date was 19 September 1864.

This first engagement between Sheridan and Early is now known as the Third Battle of Winchester, or the Battle of Opequon Creek in northern histories. Perhaps no town was more fought over during the Civil War than Winchester, Virginia. Founded in 1744 and named after the famous city in Hampshire County, England, Winchester changed hands over seventy times during the war. It was of key military importance: Whoever controlled Winchester controlled the northern access in and out of the Shenandoah Valley. By September of 1864, two battles had already been fought within the city limits; each a Confederate victory. The third and final battle, however, saw the Union fortunes victorious at last. Today the battlefield area northeast of the city is fast being encroached upon by Winchester's suburban sprawl; soon what was the battlefield terrain will not be recognizable on account of the new homes and industrial parks.

Sheridan began his movement on Winchester before dawn the morning of September 19. Leaving Berryville, he crossed the Opequon Creek and headed along what is now Route 7 towards Winchester. Cavalry led the advance, with the VI and XIX Corps following. The XIX Corps fanned out in two lines of battle along the north of the Berryville Pike, with Birge's Brigade on the far right of the first line.

About one mile past the creek the road enters Berryville Canyon, where it is bordered on both sides by steep hills. These hills slowed the Union advance. Further complicating matters were the bumbling efforts of the VI Corps, who brought their entire supply train along with their advance. It created a huge traffic jam that blocked the advance of the XIX Corps and allowed the Confederates to prepare themselves for the battle and counter-attack. Throughout the morning of the 19th, Sheridan's forces pressed their attack, and by noon had emerged out of the west end of the Berryville Canyon. General Birge's brigade in particular performed notably. In his official report division commander General Grover wrote,

Upon the arrival of General Birge's brigade to an advantageous position, and in prolongation of the line held by the troops on the left, it was ordered to halt and lie down and await orders, but having driven the enemy from his first line, in the noise and excitement of the battle...they were for a time unable to restrain the impetuosity of the ranks, and the whole brigade charged as a man and drove the enemy some 300 yards beyond where its flanks were supported or could at that time receive the proper support. Receiving a fire of artillery and small-arms upon front and flanks, of course it was obliged to retire.[6]

Two views of the starting-point for Sheridan's attack in the Battle of Third Winchester: The Opequon Ford, Berryville Pike as it was, above, and as the creek and area appear today, below.

Berryville Pike (now U.S. Route 7) as it cuts through the Berryville Canyon today, above, and the ground held by the XIX Corps in the afternoon of 19 September 1864, below.

The Confederate forces had struck back in a fierce counterattack that halted, then temporarily forced back the Union men. Losses were heavy among Union regiments, including the 14th New Hampshire. One of its losses was the regiment's commander, Col. Gardiner, who suffered a mortal wound. The historian later recalled,

> The charge of the Fourteenth—holding the right of the line—at the battle of the Opequan was a remarkable performance from any standpoint of criticism. Losing one third of its number in thirty minutes, the regiment advanced persistently until all semblance of formation was destroyed; and the scattered remnants retreated only on repeated orders.[7]

First Brigade commander General Birge's report sheds further light on the activity of the 14th New Hampshire during this phase of the battle:

> ...[this brigade]...marched through Berryville to within two miles of Winchester, and at 11 a.m. was assigned position...from right to left as follows: Fourteenth New Hampshire Volunteers, Colonel Gardiner; Twenty-Sixth Massachusetts, Colonel Farr; Twelfth Maine, Lieutenant-Colonel Ilsley; Fourteenth Maine, Colonel Porter; and Seventy-Fifth New York, Lieutenant-Colonel Babcock. A strong skirmish line was advanced through and to the edge of a piece of woods in front of the position.... At 11:45 am received orders to move on the enemy, and immediately advanced through the woods before mentioned and into an open field about 500 yards in width; crossed this field under an artillery and infantry fire from the enemy in position in a belt of woods in front and extending to the right, and when within 200 yards charged with fixed bayonets at double-quick. Broke his line on the entire front of the brigade and drove him through and out of the woods. As the troops entered the woods I was ordered by General Grover to halt and hold that position and not to go farther into the woods, but the charge was so rapid and impetuous and the men so much excited by the sight of the enemy in full retreat before them it was impossible to execute the order, and the whole line pressed forward to the extreme edge of the timber, some 300 yards beyond the enemy's original position and to his rear on both flanks. The brigade was now far in advance of our own line and subjected to a severe and concentrated enfilading fire of artillery and infantry from the right and infantry from the left. In front the enemy were retreating in great confusion, immediately and simultaneously threw and heavy force on each flank. Meantime our forces on my left had been forced back, the movement commencing to the left and extending till it had reached the right of the Third Brigade. Under these circumstances, to hold the position was impossible, and the brigade fell back to the original skirmish line.[8]

Badly hurt, the 14th New Hampshire along with other regiments of Grover's division retired from the fight as other units, such the XIII Corps, moved forward to recapture the advantage. Sheridan's vastly superior force soon reversed the Confederate advance and forced them to retreat to a defensive perimeter on the northeast corner of Winchester. Sheridan's army, with VI Corps along the Berryville Pike (at what is now US Interstate 81) and VIII Corps moving in from the northeast, boxed Early's army in and forced it to retreat. It was the first of several defeats Early would suffer in the coming month, and it insured Union control of the northern entrance to the Shenandoah Valley once and for all. Sheridan had suffered over a thousand more casualties than Early's 3,921, but while Sheridan's losses only amounted to one-eighth of his army, Early had lost an irreplaceable fourth of his army at Winchester.[9]

In its first serious taste of battle, the 14th New Hampshire and its sister units in Birge's Brigade had performed well. But it had suffered high casualties. In Pierce's company six men had been wounded (including the captain and first lieutenant), four captured, and three killed. It was the costliest battle of the war for Pierce's company. Within the regiment, the slain Colonel Alexander Gardiner was succeeded by Col. Carroll Wright.[10]

Events prohibited the 14th from grieving long over its losses, however. Three days later Sheridan's forces again outdid Early's, this time twenty miles to the south. Following his defeat at Winchester, Early had retreated to Fisher's Hill. Here a series of hills forms a narrow, natural guard to the northern entrance of the Shenandoah Valley. With an observation post high atop "Three Top Mountain,"

Colonel Alexander Gardiner, commander of the 14th New Hampshire at the Battle of Third Winchester, was mortally wounded there and died three weeks later.

CAPT. WM. A. FOSGATE.

LIEUT. JESSE A. FISK.

CAPT. WM. H. CHAFFIN.

LIEUT. HENRY S. PAUL.

LIEUT. M. S. WEBSTER.

LIEUT. A. B. COLBURN.

Officers of the 14th slain at Third Winchester—two of whom, Captain
William Chaffin and Lieutenant Henry Paul—were from Franklin
Pierce's company.

Two views—then, above, and today, below, of the north slope of Fisher's Hill, from Tumbling Run Creek along the Valley Pike, which was the focal point of the diversionary attack by the XIX Corps in the Battle of Fisher's Hill.

the northern tip of the Massanutten Mountain of the Blue Ridge Mountain chain, Early could spot any Union troops moving south from Winchester. Early's only weakness was that his forces were spread awfully thin: 11,000 men trying to hold a four-mile front against Sheridan's 30,000-man army.

The three-to-one advantage proved the Confederate's undoing. Using a night march to conceal his movements from the observers on Three Top Mountain, Sheridan split his force. The main body of his force—the XIX and VI Corps—would launch a frontal attack, hoping to direct Early's attention directly north and away from his flanks. Meanwhile, Crook's VIII Corps would circle west and strike Early's left flank.

The plan worked flawlessly. The VI and XIX Corps held Early's attention while Crook's Corps smashed into the weak Confederate left. Crook's troops overwhelmed the cavalry troops under General Lomax, while Rickett's division of VI Corps drove into the middle of the Confederate line, splitting Early's forces.

The rout was on. Early's battered army fled in haste from its positions and began a long, hasty, dismal retreat up the Shenandoah Valley, with the now very aggressive Sheridan always nipping at his heels. The retreat did not end until more than eighty miles later, with the graybacks south of Staunton.

General Early and the South never again threatened the Union borders. Sheridan's two victories climaxed a month of good news for the Union that had begun with Sherman's conquest of Atlanta. Within the space of those few weeks, any hopes of dislodging Lincoln from the Presidency and forcing a negotiated settlement were, for all intents and purposes, totally shattered.

With the Valley now safely in Union hands, Sheridan proceeded to implement the second half of his assignment: the thorough elimination of the Shenandoah as a source of Confederate supplies and avenue of invasion to the North. Sheridan about-faced on October 6 and began his work of turning one of the most scenic, bountiful valleys in America into a "barren waste," as Grant had instructed him. Under the brilliant autumnal foliage of the surrounding mountains, Sheridan applied a scorched-earth policy which implemented devastation that rivaled that of Sherman's forthcoming "March to the Sea" in Georgia. Two nights and forty miles later, Sheridan wired Grant with the following report:

> I have destroyed over 2,000 barns filled with wheat, hay, and farming implements; over 70 mills filled with flour and wheat; have driven in front of the army over 4,000 head of stock, and have killed and issued to the troops not less than 3,000 sheep. [11]

The terrible carnage continued over the following week. Witnesses were shocked at the level of destruction. Smoke from burning buildings and harvested crops blackened the skies. Slave and slave-owners alike fled in fear and for simple want of common necessities, for Sheridan had left nothing for them to go home to. So great were the Union atrocities that even now, 125 years later, descendants still recall the horror their ancestors experienced:

> Our ancestor was out milking the cows one morning when the soldiers came. They burned the barn and killed the cattle. They begged for them to spare the milk, so they could feed the children. But the soldiers spilled the milk on the ground, too.[12]

This was total war, of a kind not seen before. It broke all the accepted bounds of centuries of Christian just-war tradition which regulated how armies were to conduct wars. For Lee's troops, hunkered down in their trenches in Petersburg, it portended a winter of hunger and starvation.

Early followed Sheridan's plundering army down the Valley, but was totally helpless to stop the destruction. The best he could do was annoy Sheridan's rear guard with hit-and-run attacks by his cavalry. But it was not long before the Union beast turned on its pesky nuisance. On October 9, five miles south of Strasburg, at the little town of Tom's Brook, Sheridan ordered two of his cavalry divisions—one General George Armstrong Custer's division of Michigan Wolverines—to turn swiftly about and set upon the Confederate cavalry. The result was another humiliation as the Union cavalry chased the fatigued Southerners ten miles back up the Valley.

His work of devastation complete, Sheridan rested his troops the next day north of the entrance to the Valley just outside the town of Strasburg. For his headquarters, Sheridan commandeered Belle Grove, the lovely plantation home of the Hite family a few miles south of Middletown. His troops camped in front of it, the VI behind XIX Corps along the northern banks of Cedar Creek and west of the Valley Pike (Route 11), the VIII Corps on the east side of the pike. The 14th New Hampshire, along with the rest of the First Division of the XIX Corps, occupied an open, rolling plain in front of Belle Grove Plantation, with its east flank anchored on the pike. The Second Division continued the XIX Corps line on the right, curving back from Grover's Division to Meadow Brook, a small stream that runs parallel to the Valley Pike. Early and his men still lingered just beyond range. They reoccupied the Fisher's Hill area from which they had been routed just three weeks before. Early's battle-depleted forces were given a much-needed injection of strength by the recent arrival of an infantry division and cavalry brigade from Lee's army at Petersburg.

For Pierce and his comrades of the Fourteenth, it was a welcome rest after an exhilarating, triumphant campaign. After two years of tedious non-combat service, they had participated in a glorious campaign which, in the long stretch of war, was a key Union victory. In the cool, crisp autumn days, under a canopy of autumn reds, oranges, and yellows on the surrounding mountains, it was indeed a wonderful time to be in a winning army. Little did they know that a near-disaster awaited them, only days away.

Reinforced by the return of former units to his command from Lee's army, Early sought to reverse the humiliating defeats of the past month and keep Sheridan from sending some of his troops to help out Grant at Petersburg. On the 13th of October his men occupied Hupp's Hill, a ridge overlooking Sheridan's position midway between Strasburg and Belle Grove Plantation. A Union attack on the hills failed,

The area around Belle Grove plantation then, above, and today, below, the site of the Battle of Cedar Creek.

and Sheridan decided to recall the elements of the VI Corps which had been released to rejoin the Army of the Potomac.

Sheridan, meantime, was called back to Washington to confer with Secretary of War Edwin Stanton and Grant on future plans. Leaving the 16th, he received word of a possible large rebel force under General Longstreet coming to assist Early. Intentionally sent by Early as a decoy message to force Sheridan to retreat, Sheridan reacted in the opposite manner by positioning his cavalry to the west of his infantry corps to cut off a flanking maneuver in that direction. As a result, the left side of his position, VI Corps, was bereft of significant observation capability, leaving it vulnerable to a surprise attack.

At this point Early had to act or retreat. The devastated Shenandoah Valley could not support his army much longer. He decided on a daring night march and dawn attack in which his army would be divided into four columns. Two would attack the VI Corps positions from the east, another from the south, and the fourth column would move alongside the Valley Pike to attack XIX Corps, right where Grover's First Division was located. All four were to converge on their assigned targets at 5:00 am, on the 19th of October. Meanwhile, far to the west at Cupp's Ford, Confederate cavalry were to tie down Union cavalry and prevent them from entering the main battle to the south.

As the Confederates made their plans on the 18th, the Union forces rested easy in their positions. The memoirs of one cavalry officer recalled the beauty of the season the day before battle:

> The 18th of October in the Shanandoah Valley was such a day as few have seen who have not spent an autumn in Virginia; crisp and bright and still in the morning; mellow and golden and still at noon; crimson and glorious and still at the sun setting; just blue enough in the distance to soften without obscuring the outline of the mountains, just hazy enough to render the atmosphere visible without limiting the range of sight.[13]

The men in blue were certain that their position was impregnable and that Early's army was too weak after the whipping they had given them the last month to do any harm. It was a classic instance of assuming away the enemy's capabilities and planning for the best-case scenario. Their complacency proved costly to them the next morning. All through the night Early's columns marched toward their dawn jump-off positions. Still, not all Confederate columns were in place when, at 5:00 am, General Kershaw's division struck from the south with a volley and a roaring rush into the VIII Corps camp. Minutes later, the two Confederate columns coming from the east under Generals Gordon and Ramseur linked up with Kershaw's division against the half-asleep men of VIII Corps.

The effect was total surprise for the Rebels, total panic for the Yankees. Whole regiments simply dissolved within minutes as their positions were overrun and the men, some only half-dressed, were taken prisoner or scurried away for safety. Here and there a regiment would offer some resistance, but within a half-hour the VIII

Belle Grove Plantation then, above, and today, below. The house served as Sheridan's headquarters before the Battle of Cedar Creek.

Corps simply ceased to exist as an organized fighting force.

On the other side of the Valley Pike, the XIX Corps was a little more prepared for the Confederate onslaught. The noise of the battle on their left had awakened them; in addition, several units had been ordered up during the night to be ready to set out at dawn on reconnaissance maneuvers. Luckily, too, the fourth Confederate column, under General Wharton, had delayed in jumping off at the right time and so had lost the element of surprise the other columns had obtained. Taking command of the battle, XIX Corps commander Emory attempted hastily to organize the troops into some semblance of order to meet the onrushing attackers west of the pike. He turned his corps, plus whatever units of VIII Corps were available, parallel to the pike to meet the oncoming enemy. General Henry Birge, reporting for the wounded division commander General Grover, recalled the events as they unfolded:

> As the day dawned the enemy appeared in strong force on the high ground on the left of our position, from which he had forced back the Eighth Corps and rapidly advanced, his lines extending from the creek to our left and rear as far as could be seen through the smoke and prevailing fog. The troops on the left, thus attacked in front and flank, made a stubborn resistance, and on the line of the Third Brigade a hand-to-hand conflict ensued.... At the same time a battery opened on our lines from

"The Surprise at Cedar Creek," a war-time sketch of the Confederate attack on the XIX Corps the morning of October 22, 1864.

the left and another from the high ground in front and on the opposite side of the creek. Pressed by an overwhelming force, and having already lost very heavily, our line was forced back, retiring in good order, but leaving some prisoners in the hands of the enemy....

In the meantime the First Brigade and that part of the Second Brigade not engaged were holding their respective positions, but losing from infantry and artillery fire from front, flank, and rear. By order of General Grover they now fell back, the First Brigade along the line of works, forming a new line on the crest of the hill to the right and perpendicular to the original line, and holding it until turned by the enemy, when it fell back to the hill previously occupied by a brigade of First Division. Making a short stand here, it was again pressed back, and again made a stand in an open field, with the Fourth Brigade on its left; having, in the efforts made to check the advance of the enemy, lost severely in killed and wounded and some prisoners....[14]

The 14th's regimental historian noted the valor of the men of the 14th New Hampshire during the chaos of the dawn fighting:

At Cedar Creek, with the enemy on three sides, in the midst of indescribable confusion, the regiment fought on both sides of its breastworks, changed fronts while almost surrounded, and formed new lines at every command. Its signal steadfastness caused the brigadier to rally his shattered brigade on the colors of the Fourteenth New Hampshire.[15]

For all their valor, it was too little, too late. The three attacking columns, now joined by the fourth under Wharton, pressed home their advantage. The shattered Union brigades retreated, first back to the plantation home, then further north and west. For the VIII Corps the retreat was a simple rout; the XIX Corps managed to maintain a little better organization throughout the morning's disaster.

By 8:00 am the Confederates had pushed the Union forces two miles from their original campsites in front of Belle Grove Plantation. Their attack was slowing down: due to stiffening resistance, led by the VI Corps, which had had ample time to organize lines of battle for the onrushing attackers. Some of these troops, stationed just south of Middletown, were putting up such a terrific fight that Early mistook it for the whole of the VI Corps. Slowly, grudgingly, the VI Corps gave ground until it formed a strong defensive position about a mile north of Middletown by 11:00 am.

A second factor also set in which slowed the Rebel's advance: many Confederate soldiers were stopping to ransack the now deserted Union camps. Poorly clothed and poorly supplied, these men eagerly looted whatever clothes, food, and other supplies they could get their hands on.

Against the wishes of his officers to continue pressing the advantage, Early stopped to reorganize his units. He also became aware of Union cavalry massing on his right flank; his cavalry units under General Rosser had failed to execute their part of the plan of tying down the Union cavalry. This left the cavalry corps of

Sheridan's army free to operate at will. Early's troops occupied a line running west from the Valley Pike on the northern edge of Middletown. Here they stayed until mid-afternoon, when Kershaw and Ramseur's divisions made a weak attack against the Union center, manned by the VI Corps. Their feeble attack was quickly turned aside by a Union onslaught that reversed the entire course and outcome of the battle.

Twelve miles to the north in Winchester, where he had stayed on the 18th following his return from Washington, Sheridan woke up to the sounds of battle to the south. Saddling up and mounting his magnificent horse, Rienzi, he dashed to the battle site in a ride which became immortalized in a poem. Arriving on the field by late morning, Sheridan's return electrified his troops. He responded to their cheers with a hell-fire and brimstone sermon of his own to rally the troops back to the attack. Riding back and forth among the lines, he screamed, "God damn you, don't cheer me. If you love your country, come up to the front! God damn you, don't cheer me! There's lots of fight in you men yet! Come up, God damn you, come up!"[16]

Sheridan set about the task of reorganizing his units. The XIX Corps was reassembled on the right of his line. Further west, he stationed Custer's cavalry; Sheridan always had confidence in Custer when he got into a fight. The center of the Union line, anchoring its left on the Valley Pike, was the VI Corps. East of the pike Sheridan kept another group of cavalry units massed to menace Early's right flank.

Just after 4:00 pm, in response to the tentative Confederate attack by Kershaw and Ramseur, Sheridan swung his forces into action. As the VI Corps moved against the Confederate center, the XIX Corps swung like a hinge against the

A sketch of General Sheridan's famous ride to the rescue at the Battle of Cedar Creek.

Confederate left, thinly defended by Gordon's division. Custer used the diversion created by the XIX Corps' attack to scoot around Early's left; within minutes he was well into his rear and coming up on Belle Grove plantation.

News of Federal cavalry operating freely in their rear, plus the crushing weight of the two attacking corps, soon created a panic among Early's men like that which they had inflicted on the VIII Corps in the morning. Within the hour the entire Confederate front had collapsed and Early's army was in a pell- mell retreat back to the safety of Fisher's Hill. At the old XIX positions at Belle Grove some regiments tried to slow the advance of the Union steamroller, but to no avail.

The Battle of Cedar Creek ended as a complete rout, made worse when a bridge south of Strasburg on the Valley Pike collapsed. Early's men were forced to leave valuable artillery pieces and supply wagons behind; only the men escaped on foot. Early's army finally reached the safety of Fisher's Hill by nightfall, but withdrew further south the next day. Sheridan's Shenandoah Valley campaign was completed.

Watching this Confederate retreat through the Belle Grove plantation area were many Federal prisoners captured in the morning attack, now liberated by Sheridan's advancing army. One of the soldiers was Benjamin Franklin Pierce. He had been wounded during the morning's fighting, shot through his ankle. Unable to keep up

Meadow Brook, just west and behind Belle Grove Plantation, where Pierce bathed his injured foot during the Battle of Cedar Creek.

with the hasty Union retreat during those hours, he had dragged himself to the Meadow Brook for water. When a person is shot, hydrostatic shock resulting from the bullet's impact on the body creates a tremendous thirst. Pierce found relief in the waters of the brook; also, according to the family's oral history, he spent the rest of the day bathing his foot in it. In the medically impoverished years of the Civil War even the slightest bullet wound could and often did turn gangrenous. The running waters of the brook acted like a modern day whirlpool, cleaning out any dirt and materials that could have caused infection.

From his vantage point Pierce had a ground-level view of the Confederate flight that afternoon. Liberated, he was returned to Union lines and a field hospital. Unfortunately, his belongings were never fully returned to him. Rebel looters took everything of value he had in them, and certainly did not take the time to kindly rearrange whatever they left behind for Pierce's easy location. One item lost in the chaos of the day was Pierce's 1864 diary. Certainly he had kept one, as he had in 1863, but between the looting done by the enemy and his wounding Pierce never was able to return and locate it after the battle. Thus were lost Pierce's observations on his travels and experiences of that year. What he went through can only be reconstructed from the stories of others.

Sometime afterward, perhaps just a few days later while recuperating in a hospital, Pierce read a poem written about the victorious valley campaign of Sheridan's Army. He cut it out and carried it with him, eventually placing it in one of his diaries upon arriving home:

A Victory In The Valley

A victory in the valley, let the glorious news ring out,
How our gallant troops have conquered and the traitors put to rout.
How they broke in wild disorder when our troopers charged their flanks,
How they tried in vain to rally their thinned and broken ranks.
In the cities of the Union let the glorious news be told,
How our leaders led each charge as did the gallant knights of old;
On the mountains, in the valleys, on the hillside, on the plain,
Let the lightning flash the news, that we've triumphed once again.
That the brave old flag has triumphed and traitors sabres rust,
Their bravest leaders fallen and their banners trailed in dust.
In the cities of the South there is sorrowing today,
Sorrowing for leaders fallen and for legions swept away.
But in the broad fields of the valley rest not only rebel dead,
Many of our braves are sleeping, sleeping in their narrow bed;
Sleeping for a holy cause on the field by valor won;
May the Lord of hosts reward them for the deeds that they have done.

George Morton

CHAPTER SIX

Home At Last

General Phil Sheridan's campaign in the Shenandoah Valley was over. Sergeant Benjamin Franklin Pierce's journey through the Civil War was over, too. From the day of his wounding at Cedar Creek to his final discharge in June of the next year, Pierce's duty was confined to hospital beds as he recuperated from and adjusted to the effects of his injury.

As darkness descended on the littered battlefield about Cedar Creek, Pierce was taken to an army field hospital. This stay was only temporary; within a day or two he was transported to Baltimore's Patterson Park Hospital, arriving on the 23rd of October. Here he and other comrades from the 14th New Hampshire —including six others from his own company—received complete treatment.

Still, hospital life in Baltimore offered little pleasure, and probably much pain: Crowded conditions, the constant sight of injured men maimed for life by the terrible weapons of war— many, certainly, in far worse condition than Pierce. As sergeant and therefore the natural leader of the men from the 14th, Pierce sought to alleviate the suffering of his fellow soldiers by effecting a relocation to a hospital closer to home. One week after his arrival at Patterson he penned a letter to the governor of his state:

October 30
His Excellence J. A. Gilmore

Sir
    We the undersigned members of the 14th Regt., N. H. Vols. and at this time inmates of this hospital, would most respectfully solicit your aid in causing our transfer to our own state hospital.
    Hospital life is unpleasant and cheerless enough in any place and when far from friends and kindred it become double so, and knowing your goodness of heart, we come to you as we would to a father, feeling confident it will not be in vain.
    Pardon this liberty we have taken in addressing you, and allow us to remain your obt. servts., etc. etc.

This letter, apparently, was never mailed. Pierce intended to hand-deliver it himself, for six days later he was granted a four-week furlough to return home. According to Hattie's diary, on November 11 Franklin went to Concord; this was most likely to deliver the letter, for Hattie writes in her diary "I do hope he will have good success."

Hattie was sent word on October 31 that her husband was due home the eighth of November, but received even more welcome news a week early:

Nov. 1

Not pleasant at all but yet it has been a day
with surprise and pleasure for me. I went
over to Mr. Sargent and when I came home I
found my Frank. I am so glad he has arrived safe.

It was a welcome sight indeed for Hattie. The past two months had worn on her terribly. Her entries in her diary in July, while she was still visiting relatives in Vermont, express anxiety upon learning that Franklin was fighting along the Petersburg front:

July 26

...I guess I am glad I have two letters from
Frank I cant say that I am very glad he is on
the Potomac but I was so anxious to know where
he was. Oh dear would I be glad when this war
is over.

****

July 30

A verry pleasant day....Jo brought me a
letter from Frank. Oh dear I was so sorry to
see Petersburg in it but I guess we can't have
every thing we want in this world.

She knew a few weeks later that her husband was involved in the fighting in the Shenandoah Valley. At the end of August she had received word from Franklin that he was on the front lines:

Aug. 25

... Oh I am glad I have rec a letter from my
dear soldier Oh I am so sorry he has had to
go into the field.

Her wedding anniversary left her nostalgic and depressed over her separation from her beloved husband:

Sept. 3

This has not been so pleasant a day as I wish
it had been for it is the anniversary of my
wedding Oh where is poor Frank I wonder. 9
years have passed on wings it seems to me.

The absence of mail from Franklin heightened her anxiety over his whereabouts. The 20th finally brought a letter, but beginning the next day news of the fighting at Winchester, then Fisher's Hill, began to filter back into the village. She wrote,

Sept. 22
Did not accomplish much to day. Oh dear I am so
worried about Frank. Oh God grant that
he's spaired. Cinth is down here but she
could offer no consolation.

****

Sept. 24
Oh I do hope Frank has been spaired. I cant
tell how anxious I do feel about my precious
husban.

****

Sept. 25
Oh this has been an afful day I have been
thinking where is my poor Frank Oh I am
afraid that some thing has befallen him ....

****

Sept. 26
This has been a cold raw day I washed went to
the village to see if I could hear any thing
from my precious husban. No tidings .....

The next day Hattie finally heard from Franklin, and then a day later the terrible news came to the town of whose son had been killed or wounded in the previous week's battles:

Sept. 28 and 29
...Oh what a hard time the 14 [14th Regiment]
have had poor fellows what a sore fate they
have met with. Such a long list of killed and
wounded.

Knowing that Franklin was actively campaigning with Sheridan in the Valley caused Hattie daily turmoil. All she could do was receive letters that indicated by their date that he was alive and well as of that date, and scan the lists of dead and

73

wounded published in the town in the hope his name was not on them. Each day became an unremitting roller coaster ride of emotions: joy, sorrow, fear, thanksgiving, anxiety, relief.

Oct. 13

Oh Dear what a dreery day I did think this
morning I could not wait until night to see
the paper but it rained so Father thought he
could not go. Oh dear how I do want to hear
from my precious Frank. Oh what if he's
wounded and suffering from the want of care?
Oh I cant bear the thought.

****

Oct. 14

Oh how thankful I am tonight. I have heard
from my precious husban. Oh I thank the
heavenly Father for spairing my husband
through so many dangers.

****

Oct. 23

...Oh I do wish I knew where the being most
dear to me is. Alas I know not whether he is
on the land of the living or not. Oh when
will this cruel war end so our much beloved
ones will be home? Alas who knows the heart
ache of the poor soldier wife and who can tell
the suffering of that poor soldier no one but
those that have experienced.

The latter entry indicates that news of the engagement at Cedar Creek was filtering back to Bradford. For several days Hattie and others lived in the suspense of not knowing what had become of their loved ones, until the casualty lists were published a full week after the battle:

Oct. 28

Oh this has been a afful rainy day. I have
hear sad news indeed from my soldier. I have
hear he is wounded. Dear Frank I do hope that
you dont suffer much but I am so thankfull he

74

is spared that I cant feel so bad about his wound.

Four days later, Frank came home. The couple celebrated their reunion knowing that Frank probably would not return to duty on the front lines. Their next challenge in life would be adjusting to Franklin's wound. Hattie's first expression of fore-boding was November 6, when she noted in her diary, "I don't think his foot is any better." Franklin was out of the service, but healing from his war wound would be a long struggle in itself. To get around he had to use crutches (Hattie's diary notes this Nov. 11).

November 8 was election day. The nation turned out to re-elect Lincoln overwhelmingly. The Union successes of the Fall, beginning with Sherman's seizure of Atlanta and continuing with Sheridan's victories in the Shenandoah, quieted the nation's political discontent of the summer and robbed the Democrats, led by their candidate, former Union general George McClellan, of their main campaign issues. Across the North there was the perception that, finally, a light had appeared at the end of the tunnel of this long war. Franklin Pierce, loyal soldier that he was, voted for Abraham Lincoln "in favor of the Union and liberty," as Hattie noted in her diary. The rest of Bradford, however, voted heavily for McClellan, 197-129.[1] Today, Bradford, like the rest of New Hampshire, is a solidly Republican town. But until the Harding election in 1920, the town was consistently Democratic in its sympathies; only twice, the elections of 1896 and 1908, did the town vote for the Republican standard bearer.

On November 11 Franklin went to Concord to deliver the petition on behalf of himself and his fellow soldiers for a transfer to a New Hampshire hospital. His trip was, apparently, unsuccessful, and four days later he had to make the twenty-five mile journey again, as Hattie wrote:

Nov. 14
I dont think I shall be able to carry Frank to
the depo. Oh dear poor fellow I am so sorry
that he has to go to Concord again.

["Carrying" was by horse and buggy or, in winter, a sleigh.]

****

Nov. 15
Oh I am lonesome today and I do feel so
worried for fear Frank wont get transferred.
It will be too bad to have him go back.

Two days later Hattie sadly writes, "My worst fears were verified for my poor dear Frank have to go away. I do think it is two hard and I dont think it is right."

75

Her "poor lame soldier" (entry for Nov. 21) left that day to return to Baltimore. He was not there long before a transfer to a new hospital came through a few days after Thanksgiving: Haddington Hospital, Philadelphia.

Again, as her diary attests, Hattie and Franklin had to endure a lonely separation. Through a hard winter season, with many days "as cold as greenland," Hattie resumed her familiar routine of caring for the children, trying to make a little money, and run a household. She planned to go to Concord for Christmas December 22, but a snow storm delayed her departure until Christmas Day.

While there her diary contains an entry: "I wish the Gov had been at home. I do want Frank to come home so bad." While Franklin languished in a Philadelphia hospital, Hattie did what she could to effect his transfer north. Her entries of December 13 and 16 mention asking a "Mr. Tappans"—Mason Weare Tappen, a distinguished attorney of Bradford, former state legislator, colonel of the 1st New Hampshire Regiment, friend of the governor —to intercede for her with the Gov. Gilmore.[2]

Still, as the eventful year of 1864 came to an end, Hattie had much to be thankful for. She and Frank had endured a hard, dangerous year. They had survived. They could look forward to the eventual end of the war and Franklin's permanent return home. Her entry for the last day of the year looked forward to a better day:

> I have no more care for this year but I hope
> to spend many happy days in looking over the
> past. Hope I shall improve every year. Good
> bye.

The days certainly did get better with the New Year. Franklin received another furlough on January 10, for three weeks, and was home a day later, to Hattie's surprise. Her diary records the homecoming:

Wed. 11
Cold day. Went to the village. Took back the
drawers and brought them home. Was sewing
very busy when who should I see but my dear
husband. How glad I am.

Franklin brought even more good news: He was to be transferred, effective January 20, to a hospital in Manchester. The happy couple could finally see the end of the tunnel and the resumption of their normal lifestyle. For Hattie, it meant an end to her wartime work as a seamstress:

Fri. 14
Finished drawers today Frank says I shant do

any more.
(To which Frank added: "Yes and I mean it.")

On February 3 Frank returned to the hospital at Manchester, but was home soon again on weekend leave a week later. His duty at the hospital was light and afforded him the opportunity to make trips home. He again received a sick leave March 3, which, by Hattie's entries, he also passed on to her. She writes of having severe diarrhea and inflammation, and her irritability is reflected in the testy tone of her diary entries:

Mon. 13
Cold day. Frank went for the doctor. Was
afraid I was going to have inflammation. The
doctor came said I was pretty sick. Don't
think he knows very much.

****

Tues. 14
Quite pleasant. This is the day for the state
election. Frank rode up with the doctor. He
says I am better of course he must know. I
know I don't think the shits is verry funny.

Frank left again the next day. Hattie continued not to feel well. But her ill feeling may have been due to something else she received from Frank in addition to his illness: Hattie might have been pregnant. Hattie remarked in later years to her family that every time Frank came home from the war, she got pregnant (though if she was, the baby later miscarried). Perhaps that is behind Frank's note in her diary for January 23 and 24 —a little spat during the day, "made up as usual at night," to which Frank refers the next day, "I must say one word about our time last night. Didn't we enjoy ourselves Hat?" As winter melted away into spring, Franklin continued his duty at a Manchester hospital, breaking away frequently for trips home, particularly on weekends. Hattie wrote frequently of not feeling well to eat, tiring easily, and waking up crying—the typical symptoms of a two-month-old pregnancy.

April 6 brought wonderful news for the couple. Frank's entry in Hattie's diary marked the day:

Thurs. 6
Arrived at home today on a 30 days furlough.
Found Hat at the village with the horse so I
got a ride home. Hat says she is glad to see

77

me. Don't know about that. I was glad to see
her anyway.

The good news for Hattie and Frank preceeded still more good news from the
war front. The spring thaw marked the beginning of the final campaign against the
Confederacy. Sherman pursued Johnson into North Carolina. Grant pushed hard
against Lee's exhausted, crippled army in Virginia. On Tuesday, April 11, news
came to Bradford of the momentous event from Sunday a week before:

> Pleasant but cool. Len worked for us cutting
> wood besid the Road. I guess Hat is in better
> humor today. Good news from the Army.
> Richmond has fallen. [Franklin's entry]

In fact, not only Richmond's fall, but Lee's surrender itself was two days old
by the time news of Richmond's fall reached tiny, remote Bradford. Far quicker
was the terrible news which reached Bradford on Saturday, April 15 of the previous
night in the nation's capital. Hattie's entries for Saturday and the days following
record the sad story of Lincoln's assasination and its effect on a typical Northern
town:

> A pleasant day but rather cold. Len worked here
> in the forenoon. Frank worked for Len in the
> afternoon. Oh what sad news we have heard
> our Dier President is dead and shot
> oh dier can't be.

****

Sun. 16
Cold day. Quite a number in to day but all seem
sad. What a sad sabbath all over the Country.
Frank and I went to Mr Hacks. There is no
more room for doubt as much beloved President
is gone.

****

Weds. 19
A day of mourning all over the county. We
attended the furnel service of our much
beloved President to. Oh what a sad time. Mr.
Toffen speak well was much interested.

Thurs. 20 and Fri. 21

Finished cleaning to day. Worked afful hard
this week. We can't think of nothing but the
great loss our beloved country has met with.
The merds (*sic*) has escaped but will be caught
in all probability. I sincerly hope so.

As the end of April neared, the news from the front indicated that the long war
was finally over. But rather than causing jubilation, it seemed to evoke thoughts of
sadness at the terrible price America had paid to keep its Union together. Hattie
wrote:

Weds. 26

...We hear that the war is almost over. What
a good sound that word has to the many poor
soldiers wives and lonely mothers. And oh
wont the poor soldiers Rejoice no more Bloody
Battles.

****

Fri. 28

What sadness comes with all our joys if our
Dear President could have lived to see all his
good works fulfilled. But God is just and
doeth all things for the best. How many
lonely wives and mothers there are tonight
thinking if he could only lived until now but
they have given their lives for a holy cause.
Peace to be their ashes.

The war was over. And, on June 2, came the end to Franklin's involvement with
it:

Sat. 3

A nice day. Feel pretty well used up. Mamie
is sick over done yesterday. Frank came home
tonight with his Discharge in his pocket.
Glad to have his freedom once more.

For Franklin's old unit, the 14th New Hampshire, the end of the war came a
month later. Since January they had been serving on a new front from where

Franklin had parted company with them: with Sherman in Georgia. Following the conclusion of Sheridan's campaign in the Shenandoah, the 14th New Hampshire left shortly after the New Year for Savannah. There they served as military government over the city, which the regimental historian reported, "During the springs months this service was the most agreeable of the war."[3]

In May, following the end of the war, the 14th was part of a march on Augusta, Georgia, described as "...a romantic campaign, with its thousands of rebel soldiers roaming homeward, and the 'kingdom coming' to the exultant darkies."[4] The men from the Granite State were the first Union troops seen in Augusta. They also had the honor of hosting, as their prisoner for a day, Jefferson Davis, former president of the Confederacy. When the Union flag was raised over Fort Sumter for the first time since the start of the war, the colors of the 14th joined in the festivities. Finally, on July 7, the 14th mustered out of service at Hilton Head, S. C. At last they set sail for home. Their ship was the famous U.S.S. *Constitution*—"Old Ironsides"—which brought them to Boston (where the *Constitution* is in dock today, the oldest active ship in the U. S. Navy). The regiment was feted at a dinner in famous Faneuil Hall, then left for home to return, as Franklin already had, to "the vocations of peace."[5]

EPILOGUE

An Enduring Love

With his discharge on June 2 Benjamin Franklin Pierce left the Civil War behind him for good. He and Hattie resumed their pre-war life in Bradford. Matilda was born a year later, bringing the number of children to three, all girls. The couple would have two more children: A daughter, Abbie Louisa, born in 1872, who died in 1873, and finally a son, Thomas Wilson Pierce (1875-1935).

By the time of Matilda's birth, Franklin and Hattie had moved away from Bradford. Apparently unable to resume his work on the railroad in Bradford, or perhaps unable to support his family from its wages, Franklin took a job as a machinist in Roxbury, Massachusetts, where Franklin took a job as an engineer.

But though he had left the Civil War behind, the war had not let go of him. For the rest of his life, Franklin was dogged by the nagging effects of the illness he had contracted during his first months in the service and his ankle wound from Cedar Creek.

His ankle never recovered its former strength and hampered his efforts to move easily. Standing or walking for any length of time caused swelling. More serious were the lingering effects of his intestinal problems; they left him weakened and frequently unable to work. The medical expertise of this time did not have a name for it, but most likely Franklin had a case of spastic, perhaps even ulcerative, colitis. A neighbor of the Pierce's in Roxbury recalled his condition years afterward:

> I lived a neighbor to Benjamin F. Pierce at Boston Highlands, Mass. from Sept 1865 to Sept 1869. His health was poor all the time. He had trouble with his stomach and bowels, and was troubled with diarrhoea which disease he said he contracted in the army.[1]

A statement by Franklin, made in 1895, recounts his troubles after moving to Stoughton:

> After coming to Stoughton I was employed as a locomotive engineer until October, 1891. During this time my health was very poor. I was off duty as much as one quarter of the time...I frequently had to leave my engine and go home on account of this disability. I was at one time taken from my train and caried home sick. Oct. 1891 I was removed from my job the reason given for my Discharge was because I was sick so much. I was given a job around the Engine house at about one half the pay I received as Engineer. The work is much lighter than before but I could not do even this job were it not for the help of my son who does all my hard work for me.[2]

Benjamin Franklin Pierce in 1893, age 61.

Harriett "Hattie" Pierce in 1893, age 57.

Benjamin Franklin Pierce, in his final years.

Harriett Jane Pierce, sometime after her move to Bald Eagle Lake following Franklin's death in 1915.

Franklin and Harriett Pierce's final resting place: Pleasant Hill Cemetery, Bradford. Along with Franklin's parents on the front, the left side of the marker notes the graves of their daughters, Abbie Eva and Abbie Louisa, son Thomas on the right side, and Franklin's sister and her husband, Cynthia and Len Jameson, on the back.

Pierce qualified for and received a disability pension from the government from the date of his discharge in 1865. It was a pittance—only $4.00 a month—and in his later years Franklin applied for increases to supplement his dwindling ability to earn a living. Finally, on June 9, 1915, the old soldier passed from this life into the next. He was 83 years old. He was taken back to Bradford, where he was laid to rest in the little valley amid the beautiful hills of the New Hampshire.

Harriett Pierce survived her husband by almost ten years. Following his death, she moved west to Minnesota, where all three of her daughters had moved after their marriages. Her son, Tom, also joined her there shortly before her death. Hattie lived with her daughter, Bertha Frances Pierce. She is remembered, vaguely, by her granddaughter (Joanne Murnane) as "...a tiny, white-haired old lady with an ear horn who wore long black dresses and hid peppermint candies in her pockets." An obituary published in Stoughton after her death described her life:

> ...as the greater part of her life was spent in Stoughton, she always considered herself a New Englander. The affairs of her friends in the East were a source of never-failing interest, and the arrival of the Stoughton paper was a matter to be anticipated from week to week. Her mind, keen and alert to the last, never lost its

interest in National affairs, and last November she felt the greatest satisfaction in casting her vote for President Coolidge.[3]

Upon her death after a short illness in March 1925, Harriett Jane Pierce returned to the New England soil that she dearly loved. She was laid to rest beside "her dear husband," as she had referred to him so many times in her Civil War diary, in the beauty of the New Hampshire hills.

****

Though apart, together Franklin and Hattie faced and conquered all the challenges the war inflicted on them. They endured the pain and loneliness of separation. They bore the burden of being carried along by events over which they had little control, and the anxiety of not knowing which day might be Frank's last. When struck by the tragedy of their little daughter's death, they somehow found the courage to continue on. Following the war, when Franklin's injuries crippled him from doing full-time work, together they surmounted this obstacle as well.

It is this legacy which they left for future generations to learn from and continue. We do not create our lives from nothing; we are born into and are nurtured in family cultures which shape how we look at the world, think, and act. Families are transmitters of values, beliefs, and practices which span generations, holding them together in the remembrance of the past and inspiring hope for the future. The values exemplified in a person's life survive and continue in the lives of those who follow in succeeding generations. The significance of a story like Franklin and Hattie Pierce is not just that of a curiosity item of the past. Franklin and Hattie left for their descendants to emulate the example of an enduring love, a faithful love. This is why we remember the past, that the examples of those who have gone before us may serve as examples for us in the struggles and challenges we face today.

THE
DIARIES

THE FRANKLIN AND HATTIE PIERCE COLLECTION

In addition to the diaries, several other effects of Franklin and Hattie Pierce have been passed down through the generations of their descendents to various members of the family in the present. We have decided to present them here, as a whole, as a pictorial introduction to the diaries.

Photo #1:   A group picture of the collection of Franklin and Hattie Pierce diaries. Also included is Franklin Pierce's Bible which he used in the field. He wrote in it, "This has been my constant companion on many a lonely bivouac." A number of passages in the Bible were underlined in pencil, but too light for reproduction in this ensemble.

Photo #2:   A page, in coded message, of Franklin Pierce's 1863 diary.

Photo #3:   Hattie Pierce's diary entry for April 15, 1865, recording her reaction to the news of Lincoln's assasination:

"A pleasant day but rather cold. Len worked here in the forenoon. Frank worked for Len in the afternoon. Oh what sad news we have heard our Dier President is dead and shot oh dier can't be."

Photo #4:   14th New Hampshire Regiment medallion, with page recording the draft of the letter Pierce sent to Governor Gilmore from the hospital as background.

Photo #5:   These are toys carved from wood and bone for little Eva Pierce during Frank's absence in 1863. The little ring (forward, left) has a carved monogram: "AEP" (Abbie Eva Pierce).

Photo #6:   Hattie's pen and case.

#1 (above)

#2 (below)

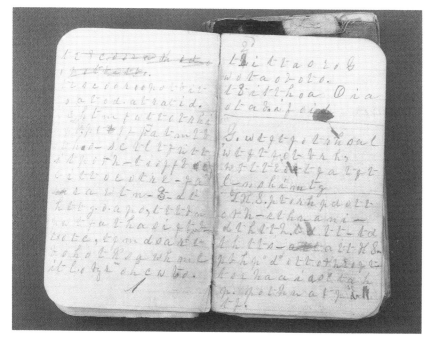

SATURDAY 15 A pleasant day but rather cold Ben worked here in fore noon. Frank worked per Ben in the after noon oh what sad News we have heard our Dea. President is dead and shot oh dea can it be

#3 (above)

#4 (below)

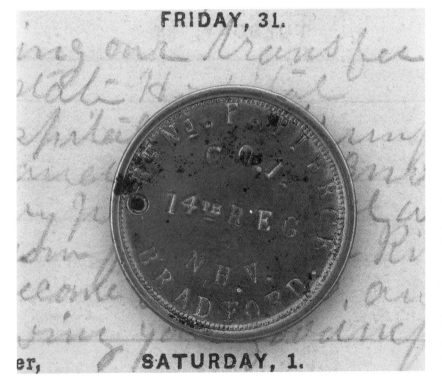

FRIDAY, 31.

SATURDAY, 1.

#5 (above)

#6 (below)

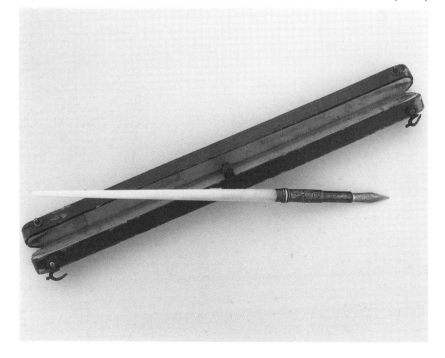

INTRODUCTION TO THE DIARIES

There are six diaries in all, recorded in 1855, 1856, 1863, 1864, 1865, and 1871. Most of the diaries (1855, 56, 1863, and the 1871) were kept by my great-greatgrandfather, Benjamin Franklin Pierce from Bradford, New Hampshire. The 1864 and 1865 diaries were recorded by Pierce's wife, Harriett (Hattie) Jane Graves Pierce, during their separation while serving in the Civil War.

The transcripts which follow are for the three diaries kept during the war years—1863, 1864 and 1865.

There is, however, some useful information in some of the other diaries. In the 1856 diary, for example, there are notations that make reference to people in various companies. Some pages appear to be torn off, presumably to serve as notes. Also, there is a draft of a letter written to Governor Gilmore of New Hampshire asking that the men from his Company be transferred to a hospital closer to home. Pierce most likely took this book with him when he went back to his unit following his leave in November 1864. There are several pages in the back of this diary which he has redated starting December 1, 1864. The transcript of this information is included at the end of this collection.

In the diary from 1871, Pierce's veteran's pension registration number, "Pension Certificate Number 49,997," is recorded in the front of the book.

S. C.

Introduction to the Diary of B. F. Pierce, 1863

Of all the diaries in the Pierce collection, none is shabbier than that of 1863. The book itself is tattered; the entries are sparse and nearly illegible. Affixed to the back cover is fragment of another notebook. It is a tantalizing little notebook, filled with a list of numbered names and containing several pages of what looks like some type of code.

On the inside front cover is written: "B. F. Pierce, Poolsville, MD." Upside down on the flyleaf the following names and companies are listed:

> A.C. Bailey, Co.H.,
> W. Williams, " "
> H. Reason, " B
> W. McMahan, " "
> M. Gorman, " C
> A.A. Adams, " C.

In the little notebook fragment is another list of names and numbers and the code. The names are listed at the end of this diary section.

After several blank pages following these entries, there are three pages of what look like codes. I have been unable to translate this information.

S. C.

B.F. Pierce's 1863 diary

January 1863

Thursday, Jan. 1
A cold day. In camp all day doing nothing. Bought this book of the _nther [illegible] today and got trusted for it.

Friday, Jan. 2
In camp all day at Poolsville doing nothing. Warm in the daytime but cold at night.

Saturday, Jan. 3
Quite cold in the morning but warm towards noon. Co. Sergent of the guard today.

Sunday, Jan. 4
Wrote a letter to Sister Lou and one to Len. A pleasant day with some signs of rain.

Commenced a letter to Hattie.

Monday, Jan. 5
A fine day. At work all day on our stockade; got it done just before dress parade and got moved into it. Col Juett takes command of this Brigade today.

Tuesday, Jan. 6
Raining all the afternoon. Paymaster came last night. Quite a sharp fight today between cavelry and Battery got a letter from Hattie today and one from Len. Sent one to H.

Wednesday, Jan. 7
A cold day, got paid off today, amount received 9.45 cts. Went over to town today. No mail today.

Thursday, Jan. 8
A stormy day commenced snowing about 10 A.M. On Provost guard at headquarters. Sergt of the guard. Half past nign at night
Snowing a very little. Having cleared off about noon and quite pleasant until sundown. No mail.

Friday, Jan. 9
A pleasant but cold day, no mail today. Like to have froze to death last night, no tents for guard to sleep in at Headquarters. Relieved at 9 1/2.

Saturday, Jan. 10
Snowing in the morning but turns to rain before noon. Got a letter from Hattie today. Quite a warm rain for the season.

Sunday, Jan. 11
Some rain today. Wrote to Hat and to Len. In camp all day. Sent 3 dollars to Hat.

Monday, Jan. 12
A pleasant day. Fateague duty today. Went down on the Conrads Ferry road to take down a stable with Lieut Chandler and fifty men. Five men deserted last night.

Tuesday, Jan. 13
A pleasant day. Out on battalian drill today for the first time for 3 weeks. Had some fresh beef for dinner fryd.

Wednesday, Jan. 14
Some signs of rain in the morning. Five men skiddoo from Co. [illegible] C. Had some liver for breakfast. Captain started for Washington.

Thursday, Jan. 15
Some rain last night. Cloudy with high winds and sign of rain. Drawing clothing. Drew one pr. pants. Wrote to Hat and sent picture. Got a mail, but no letter for me.

Friday, Jan. 16
Raining hard all night. Clears off about 9 O.c and turns cold toward night. Had some fryd potatoe for super. The old stove smoked awfuly. Cut a hole in the door and put a peace of stove pipe in to give it a good draft.

Saturday, Jan. 17
A cold day an quite windy. Hard tack and coffee for breakfast. Had some potatoes and pork for dinner. Got a letter from Len.

Sunday, Jan. 18
A fine day. Got up at five O.c and built a fire. Had hard tack for breakfast. Wrote to Len. Our stove came today. Capt. Chaffin got back from Washington. Huntoons box came, had some good things to eat.

Monday, Jan. 19
A pleasant day. In camp all day. Battallion drill fore and afternoon.

Tuesday, Jan. 20
A cold raw day and some signs of rain. Got a letter from Hattie mailed the [looks like 12th or 15th]. Not very well today and didn't go out for drilling or a paper from home.

Wednesday, Jan. 21
A wet day. Rained hard all night. Drew five days rations for the company. Commenced a letter to Hattie. Had some beef steak for dinner.

Thursday, Jan. 22
A wet day. Wrote to Hattie. Mail come today but not letter for me. In quarters all day doing nothing.

Friday, Jan. 23
Clearing off this morning. Huntoons on duty today in town. Went over and drew fresh beef for the company.

Saturday, Jan. 24
A pleasant day and quite warm. Got a letter from Hattie. Went over to town on the afternoon. Some signs of rain toward night. A rumor that Burnside had taken Lee or Longstreet and their divisions is going the rounds.

Sunday, Jan. 25
A warm morning with some signs of rain. Inspection of arms at 10 O.c Drew one vol potatoes for co. Wrote to Hattie.

Monday, Jan. 26
Some signs of rain in the morning but breaks away before noon. Left camp at 9 for picket duty on Conrads Ferry road. Some signs of rain at sundown. [There are lines crossed out at the end of this entry and re-entered below]:

Tuesday, Jan. 27
E. O. Marshall died last night at 10 O.c. A wet morning. No mail for me. [Lines crossed out at the end of this entry are re- entered for Weds. the 28th regarding Paul and Huntoon started for Washington....]

Wednesday, Jan. 28
Snowing all day but melts as fast as it comes. Paul and Huntoon started for Washington with Marshall's body. In our quarters all day doing nothing but playing euchre and seven up. Wrote a few lines to Hat.

Thursday, Jan. 29
Very stormy in the forenoon but clears away towards night. Wrote a few lines and sent to Hattie. About 6 inches of snow. Mail come but no letter for me.

Friday, Jan. 30
Not quite so cold today but looks like a storm. Morrill went out and got some boards to build bunks of to be delivered tomorrow.

Saturday, Jan. 31
A pleasant day. Building bunks today. Regimental inspection today. Got a letter from Len today said that Hattie was sick.

February 1863

Sunday, Feb. 1
A warm pleasant day. Drew five days rations. Sent a letter to Len today and one to Geroge Peaslee. Woodbury over to headquarters on guard.

Monday, Feb. 2
A clear cold day. Drew five days rations of potatoes. Out on Company drill afternoon for the first time in two weeks.

Tuesday, Feb. 3
A cold day. In camp all day. Mail today but no letter for me. Wind blowing hard all day.

Wednesday, Feb. 4
A cold raw day. Went into the woods and choped wood all day. Detail for wood chopers: Lieut N. L. Chandler, Sergts A. W. Richardson, R. Huntoon, T. J. Morrill, B. F. Pierce. No letter from home for me.

Thursday, Feb. 5
Snowing in the morning and a cold raw day but grows warmer towards night and turns to rain. No word from Hattie.

Friday, Feb. 6
Raining in the morning but some signs of clearing about 10. Up with Powers and Currier last night. Powers went to Hospital. H. L. Paul sick. No word from Hattie.

Saturday, Feb. 7
A fine day but very muddy walking. Huntoon went on picket. No word from Hattie. Two company drills today. Currier no better.

Sunday, Feb. 8
A fine day but muddy in camp all doing nothing. Got a letter from Len. Hattie some better. Some signs of rain towards night.

Monday, Feb. 9
A fine day. Wrote to Hattie today. Out for company drill twice today. Gillingham got his discharge and started for home today.

Tuesday, Feb. 10
A pleasant day. Had two battallion drills today. Woodbury quite sick today. Drew fresh beef and hard tack for co. Got a letter from Hattie and one from Len. Hattie better. H. L. Paul better. Wrote a letter to Hattie.

Wednesday, Feb. 11
Looks this morning as though it would storm. Put the letter to Hattie in the office. Woodbury no better. Snowing at 3 O.c Had some beef steak for dinner. Hard tack and coffee for supper. Drew five days rations.

Thursday, Feb. 12
A warm day and some signs of rain. Got a letter from sister Lou. Said all were well.

Friday, Feb. 13
Quite warm in the morning but grows cold towards night. Battallion drill twice today.

Saturday, Feb. 14
Not a very cold day and some signs of rain in the morning; but grows colder towards night. Woodbury got a letter tonight. Says Hattie is better. No letter for me.

Sunday, Feb. 15
A pleasant day. In camp all day. Quite muddy under foot. Wrote a letter to Hattie and one to Len.

Monday, Feb. 16
A fine day. Sent my two letters this morning. No battallion drill today. Company drill twice. Some signs of a storm.

Tuesday, Feb. 17
A stormy day. Snowing quite hard in the morning. Went on picket today. Snowing at sundown. About five inches on the ground. Powers died about 5 a.m.

Wednesday, Feb. 18
Looks as though it would storm this morning. About six inches of snow. Countersign last night was Madrid. Begins to rain at 2 O c. Peck died about 4 p.m.

Thursday, Feb. 19
A wet day and bids fair to continue so for some time. Look towards night as though it would clear off. Wrote to Hattie and recd a long letter from her and she says she is getting better.

Friday, Feb. 20
Cleared off last night and is quite cool. Went over to the mass camp for an ambulance to carry Peck body to Adamstown on its way home. It started about 8 1/2. Sent a letter to Hattie.

Saturday, Feb. 21
A very pleasant day but a cold wind. Went about a mile after straw. Lost my pocket-book but nothing in it but three postage stamps and my corporals warrent. Got a letter and two papers from Len.

Sunday, Feb. 22
A stormy day, snowing nearly all day and cold and windy towards night; about 5 inches of snow. On camp guard today. Segt. of the guard. Wrote a letter to Hat; one to Len and one to sister Lou.

Monday, Feb. 23
A very pleasant day but quite cool. Put my letters in the office.

Tuesday, Feb. 24
A pleasant day. Nothing new today but some signs of rain. No letters from home.

Wednesday, Feb. 25
A pleasant day. No news today. Some signs of a storm. Wrote a few lines to send home.

Thursday, Feb. 26
A rainy day. No news today. Got a letter from Hattie and one from Len. Wrote a few lines to Hat.

Friday, Feb. 27
Looks as though it would be a rainy day this morning but clears away about noon. Drew 200 lbs fresh beef today.

Saturday, Feb. 28
A pleasant day but quite cool. Inspection of arms today and mustered in for our pay. Mail today but no letter for me.

March 1863

Sunday, March 1
Raining in the morning but clears off before noon and quite cool. Wrote a letter to Hattie. Drew four days rations for the company.

Monday, March 2
A pleasant day. Company drill in fore noon and battallion drill after. Had quite mimic fight with blank cartridges. Some signs of rain towards night.

Tuesday, March 3
Quite a hard shower last night but warm and pleasant in the morning, but clouds up toward noon and some squaly. Wm. Paige wouldent come out to drill and was taken out. No mail tonight.

Wednesday, March 4
A pleasant day but cool high winds. Grows colder towards night. Drew four boxes of hard bread.

Thursday, March 5
A pleasant day but clouds up toward night. On picket snowing and hailing at 9 p.m. Countersign Rhodillen [could he mean Rhode Island?] Lieut Adams Lieut of guard. Went to station on conrads ferry road.

Friday, March 6
Storming some in morning but stops about 8 a.m. Releaved about 9 a.m. found two letters for me when I got to camp, one from Hattie and one from Len. Got a letter from G. Peaslee at night.

Saturday, March 7
A wet day in camp all day doing nothing.

Sunday, March 8
Raining in the morning but clears away towards night. Wrote to Hat and to Len. Raining again at night.

Monday, March 9
Clear and cool. Went over to town and got a picture taken. Man in Co. H got shot while after straw. Hit on the hand and through leg. Didn't find the one that shot him.

Tuesday, March 10
Raining in the morning. Snowing at ten. Wrote a letter to Hattie and sent deguerreotype in it. Raining again at night.

Wednesday, March 11
A pleasant morning but cool. Some snow on the ground. Drew rations for company.

Thursday, March 12
A pleasant day but cool. Some signs of rain or snow. Got two letters from Hattie. L. J. Morrell trys to get a furlough but don't succeed.

Friday, March 13
A cold day but pleasant. In camp all day doing nothing.

Saturday, March 14
A pleasant day but some signs of a storm. Got a letter from Hattie. Chandler got back.

Sunday, March 15
A cold stormy day. Went up and carried the boys' dinner to headquarters. Drew rations for company.

Monday, March 16
A stormy morning. Pane started with Cloughs body for Washington. Took boys breakfast to headquarters.

Tuesday, March 17
A pleasant but rather cool. In camp all day. Lieut Brown got an honorable discharge and started for home this morning.

Wednesday, March 18
Pleasant in the morning but some signs of a storm. Went up on provost guard at night. Six prisoners there now. Didn't sleep any all night.

Thursday, March 19
A pleasant day but cool. Some signs of a storm. Got a letter from Hattie and one from J. Coon.

Friday, March 20
Pleasant but cool and some signs of a storm.

Saturday, March 21
A pleasant day but cool. Got a letter from Hattie tonight. All well at home. The letter was mailed at East Washington. Said she was going over the next day after she wrote.

Sunday, March 22
A very warm pleasant day. The warmest day we have had this spring but some signs of rain towards night. Wrote a letter to Hattie.

Monday, March 23
Some signs of rain this morning. On camp guard today. Corporal of the guard. Ten at night very dark and raining some. Had stewed beans for dinner. D. J. Pillsbury quite sick with the measles.

Tuesday, March 24
A pleasant day. Got a letter from Len. Some signs of a storm towards night.

Wednesday, March 25
A stormy morning but clears off about noon. Quite warm. Some light showers in the afternoon.

Thursday, March 26
Quite cool and windy. Went for a target shute. Drew rations for six days for com. Got a letter from Hattie tonight. Said all were well.

Friday, March 27
A very pleasant day. Had a good game of Ball today. Battalion drill. Had some plank katridges. Sent a letter to Hattie. Some signs of rain tonight.

Saturday, March 28
Commenced raining about four o.c. this morning and bids fair to be a rainy day. No letter from Hattie.

Sunday, March 29
A cold day and quite windy. In camp doing nothing. Wrote a letter to Hattie. Drew 185 lbs fresh beef today.

Monday, March 30
A pleasant day. Preparing for monthly inspection, cleaning guns and equipment. Took H. L. Browns place as corporal of relief no. 2 at eleven p.m.

Tuesday, March 31
Snowing quite hard in the morning but clears off about noon and quite pleasant. Mostly in our quarters today on account of the weather. Got a letter from Hattie. All well.

April 1863

Wednesday, April 1
A cold day and quite windy.

Thursday, April 2
A pleasant day but some signs of a storm. Right wing recd orders to march in the morning. Wrote to Hattie.

Friday, April 3
A pleasant day. Struck our tents and bid farewell to Poolsville at 10 o.c. Co. B & D stoped at Seneca. A & C at muddy branch and Co. I at Great Falls. Arrived there 8 1/2. Slept on the boat.

Saturday, April 4
A cold day but pleasant. Picked out our ground and began to build our tents out of wood. Some signs of a storm. Got up three double tents.

Sunday, April 5
Snowing quite hard in the morning. Nearly 12 inches of snow on the ground at nigh

o.c. Clears off cold a little after noon. Started for Poolsville about 4 p.m. on a boat after what lumber we left.

Monday, April 6
Left Edwards Ferry 12 p.m. at night. Arrived at Poolsville 3 1/2 a.m. Walk from Edwards Ferry 5 miles. Very pleasant but awful muddy. Found boys we left behind asleep in cookhouse. Couldn't get a team today to draw boards to locks.

Tuesday, April 7
A cold windy day. Left Poolsville at eight o.c. a.m. with W. & W. Howard, W. Lewis, D. C. Curriese & Hart and all the lumber I could find blonging to Co. I. Took boat at 10 a.m. Arrived at Great Falls 12 at night.

Wednesday, April 8
A pleasant day. At work around camp all day. Adjutant Gardner Quartermaster Webster & Surgeon Perkins visit us but no mail.

Thursday, April 9
A pleasant day. Cutting and clearing ground all day. Captain got his house done.

Friday, April 10
A pleasant day. Sergt of the guard today.

[No further entries occur until Thursday, May 21.]

May 1863

Thursday, May 21
Warm and dusty. Recd a letter from Hattie.

Friday, May 22
Warm, dry and dusty. Went over to the 2 Regt camp. Saw George Carter of Concord.

Saturday, May 23
A warm day. Paid off up to the first of May. Went with the Regt. about three miles for Brigade drill under Genl Martindale.

Sunday, May 24
A warm, dry day. On duty today. Camp guard. Some signs of showers in the forenoon. A little sprinkle of rain about one o.c.

[May 25-27 no entries. Then Thursday 28-30 the same entries are re-entered, as if Pierce had lost track of the days.]

Sunday, May 31
A warm, dry day. On duty today. Camp guard. A little rain afternoon.

June 1863

Monday, June 1
Warm dry and dusty with no signs of rain. No letter from Hattie.

Tuesday, June 2
Doing guard duty over at Old Capital prison as a private. Saw George Carter in the morning before leaving camp. No letter from Hattie.

Wednesday, June 3
Half past four

[Here the entries end again and there is nothing more recorded until September 24, 1863.]

September 1863

Thursday, Sept. 24
Pleasant but quite cool. Sick in camp all day. Recd a letter from Hattie.

Friday, Sept. 25
Pleasant in the morning with some signs of rain. On duty at the Old Capital prison. One hundred and twenty rebel prisoners came in today to the Old Capital Cold and lonely at 12 midnight. Capt. Mars in comp. guard.

Saturday, Sept. 26
A cold windy day. About 300 prisoners left the Old Capital prison today for Point Lookout. Relieved by Capt. Bunton at 9 o.c. Went over to the citty on pass afternoon. Saw Sr Chandler at Provost Marshalls.

Sunday, Sept. 27
A pleasant day but cool. Rec'd a letter from Hattie. [Lines crossed out: "went over to...at Provost Marshalls" from preceeding entry.] Paid 25 cts for tobacco. Wrote a letter to Hattie. Bread and milk for supper. [upside down line reads: 15 cts for milk, 5 for aples, 5 for cheese.]

Monday, Sept. 28
Very cool in the morning. Had some bread an milk for breakfast. Had bread and milk for supper.

Tuesday, Sept. 29
Quite cool in the morning, but warm towards noon. On camp guard today. The Capt. got back from N. H. this morning and Charley Comins wife came with him. Had some beef steak for dinner.

[No further entries until Tuesday, Oct. 20.]

October 1863

Tuesday, Oct. 20
Little Eva died.

[No further entries until Thursday, Oct. 29.]

Thursday, Oct. 29
Started for home today at 6 o.clock p.m. W. Paige started with me.

Friday, Oct. 30
Arrived in New York 6 1/2 a.m. and left at eight; Arrived at Clairmont 11 p.m. Put up with G. Locet.

Saturday, Oct. 31
Got left by the stage and hired Locet to carry me to Newport over took the stage there. Arrived at B. at eight and got down home about 9. Poor little Hattie was sitting by the window when she first saw me. Glad to see me god bless her.

November 1863

Sunday, Nov. 1
A home all day with Hat.

[No entries Nov. 2-4.]

Thursday, Nov. 5
Sold our steers today to J. Marshall for 70 dollars.

[No entries until Thurs., Nov. 12.]

Thursday, Nov. 12
Started for Washington. Left Hattie and all the rest crying, and I feel as tho I had left all I hold dear on Earth behind and I have. May we all need to part no more soon. God bless my wife and children.

Friday, Nov. 13 [crossed out; original entry I suspect, rewritten in lines above.]

Started for Washington this morning. Poor Hattie feels very bad and I feel as tho I hadn't [illegible] thos I had left all that I hold dear on Earth behind and so I had. God grant I may meet them again to part no more.

Saturday, Nov. 14
Arrived at Washington last night at 10. Wrote a letter to Hattie and sent two dollars in it.

[No entries Nov. 15 - 18.]

Thursday, Nov. 19
A warm, pleasant day. The Regt paid off today. Paid Sergt Morrell 50 cts, Hardy 45; Sutter 4.00. Recd from Paymaster 6 dollars. Wrote to Hattie.

Friday, Nov. 20
On duty at the Old Capital Prison. Went up and got my commutation 2.86 A pleasant day and quite warm.

Saturday, Nov. 21
In camp all day. Raining hard all day. Recd a letter from Hattie. God bless her. All well at home. Wrote a letter to Hat to send in the morning.

Sunday, Nov. 22
A pleasant morning. On duty today at the Old Capital Prison. Sent a letter with two dollars in it to Hattie.

Monday, Nov. 23
A pleasant day.

Tuesday, Nov. 24
Some rain today but clears away towards night. On camp guard today.

Wednesday, Nov. 25
A pleasant day but a cold wind. No letter from Hattie.

Thursday, Nov. 26
A pleasant day but cool. In camp all day. No letter from Hattie. Got the blues tonight.

Friday, Nov. 27
A pleasant day but some signs of rain toward night.

Saturday, Nov. 28
A rainy day, on guard in camp today. Recd a good loving letter from my dear wife and I feel better. All well at home thank God.

Sunday, Nov. 29
A pleasant day but quite cool. Wrote to Hattie today and sent 1 00 dollar and a ring. Also sent a paper to her. Wrote a letter to Ab Graves.

Monday, Nov. 30
On duty at the Old Capital Prison. Went down to see the Capt at Sixth Street wharf. Sold my dress coat to W. Welch for 12 00 dollars. He says Captain C paid 5 00 down and the balance sometime this or next month.

December 1863

Tuesday, Dec. 1
A pleasant day but cool. On duty at Guard House. Recd a letter from Hattie and one from Len.

Wednesday, Dec. 2
Pleasant but cool In camp all day after being relieved at G. H.

Thursday, Dec. 3
Pleasant but cool.

[No further entries in diary for 1863.]

In the "Memoranda" section at end of book the following entries are recorded:

Jan. 7th
Recd from Cyrus Baily $5.00 to keep for him until he wants it.

"	10th	paid him	1.00
"	16	paid	1.00
"	19	"	65
"	30	"	1.00

Feb.   3
     "   "   1.00
     "   "   25

On next page, there is a list entitled what looks like "Snipers":
No.   1   B. F. Terrill   Co   D
      2   J. F. Foster   "   "
      3   J. S. Janorin   "   "
      4   W. Boowin   "   "

                              B. F. Pierce

On the next page the following names are written:

            A. J. Congdon
            Cair of J. G. Smith

At bottom of page, list:
N. D. Riley
A. Jerrod
16. J. Bahan   Co. I
15. E. Pollard   Co. I

Inside back page:
 1   M. Mitchell,   Co. H
 2   G. W. Ludd,   Co. H
 3   E. J. Brown   "   "
 4   H. H. Smith   "   "
 5   P. Paro   "   "
 6   D. Maxwell   "   "
 7   J. W. Purle   "   "
 8   B. White   "   "
 9   G. W. Nelson   "   "
10   W. Henson   "   E
11   I. D. Orcutt   "   "
12   G. Grey   "   "
13   M. Colby   "   "
14Mr. J. Stow

On back flyleaf, names, very faded:

Harrington 12
[illegible names]
Dayton 2
Graves 4
[illegible names]
Shippy 8
Coffer 10
[illegible names]

The little booklet referred to at the beginning is affixed to the back cover of this book. The following names are written in the notebook:

34 E. C. Woodward
35 _ _ _ _ Britton
36 Mrs. _ _ _ _ Ward
37 Robert Jackson
38 [illegible]
39 [illegible]
40 L. Bryant
41 [4 lines illegible]
42
43
44
45 ? R. Reyolds
46 Mary A. G——-
47 Ewan P——-
48 Jane ?
49 Ohry Pitz———
50 ?

[inside page]
51 H. L. Johnson
52 blank
53 Clinton Britton
54 blank
55 Fr. M. Ellms
56 blank
57 M. Southworth
58 J. Dennison
59 blank
60 blank

61 G. Gray
62 blank
63 Benj Samls
64 Mary W. Monk
65 blank
66 blank
67 E. C. Mowb
68 blank
69 D. S. Hall
70 Mary W. Monk
71 A. Caflin Jr.
72 blank
73 Carrie M. Tilden
74 blank
75 Mrs. Be. Burnham
76 C. W. Sano
77. M. French
78 blank
79 blank
80 blank
81 J. D. Gowls
82 blank

Next page:
83 Alfred Dupham
84 blank
85 F. Hide
86 blank
87 E. C. Monk
88 F. M. Ellms
89 blank
90 E. F. Bryant
91 blank
92 Samben
93 blank
94 Georgie Henderson
95 M. Bailey
96 blank
97 Mills
98 blank
99 Mary W. Monk
100 H. Fitzpatrick
40 C. F. Drake

Brief Entries From 1864

In the back pages of a diary kept while Pierce was in Terre Haute in 1856, there are a number of entries dated December 1 through 7, 1864, and the transcript of a letter written to Governor Gilmore from Patterson Park Hospital. Pierce most likely brought this diary back to the hospital with him following the leave he had in November shortly after he was wounded.

The diary entries are written into a blank section of the book from September 1856.

Thursday, December 1, 1864
Record. A pleasant day but quite cool. No letter from Hattie since I left home. Sent a letter to her today. Nothing took place today worthy of note. Saw Col. Whitaker. [In the margins: Wrote to Len.]

Friday, Dec. 2
Pleasant in the morning. Paid 25 cts for postage stamps $.10 for cheese, .10 for apples. Begins to rain about 4 p.m. Get no letter from Hat yet. O why dont I get one. I am so lonely.

Saturday, Dec. 3
Today bids fair to be a wet one and lonely enough to me. The mail came but no letter for me. O what would I give to be with my wife and little ones today.

Sunday, Dec. 4
Pleasant but cool this morning. Had hash for breakfast.

Monday, Dec. 5
A pleasant day but cool. No letter from Hattie yet. I fear she is sick.

Tuesday, Dec. 6
Pleasant in the morning. Recd a letter from Hattie at noon. She is well with the exception of a sore finger. Says the children are quite well. Some signs of rain toward night.

Wednesday, Dec. 7
Raining this morning. Sun shining at 10 a.m. Raining again at noon and quite cold.

There are no further entries from this time period until the following letter in the back pages of this book on a page dated Thursday, October 30, 1856.

His Excellence J. A. Gilmore
Sir

We the undersigned members of the 14th Regt. N.H. Vols. and at this time inmates of this hospital, would most respectfully solicit your aid in causing our transfer to our own state hospital.

Hospital life is unpleasant and cheerless enough in any place and when far from friends and kindred it become double so, and knowing your goodness of heart, we come to you as we would to a father, feeling confident it will not be in vain.

Pardon this liberty we have taken in addressng you, and allow us to remain your obt. servts., etc. etc.

[On the next page]
[Nov. Wed. 5, 1856]

Pierce Bradford
Paterson Park

Sergt B. F. Pierce
Hospital Baltimore Park

Sergt B. F. Pierce
Company G 14th
Regt N. H. Vols.

[The above appears as if he were practicing writing his own name. It is scrawled, and in some cases words are repeated across the page.]

Introduction to Hattie's 1864 Diary

The diary kept by Harriet Jane Goodwin Pierce in 1864 was probably intended to be kept in 1863. The actual book is dated 1863 on the outside cover, but handwritten on the flyleaf is: "Mrs B. F. Pierce, Diary for 1864." Also, the dating of events recorded in the diary—from public events such as elections to individual events such as dates when B. F. Pierce was injured or home on leave— confirm that it was kept in 1864. The discrepency in the dates is a mystery not explained by the text.

Inside the front cover there is a list: comb, shoestrings, tobacco, hand brush, black bread, gas white, and so on. On the frontispiece is written, presumably by Frank: "Thank you dear wife for the many times I have been remembered in this book." The next page is a calendar for 1863. On the back, a note is scribbled, date unknown:

"Oh I was so glad to hear from dear Frank. Oh I thank God for sparing my precious husband but I don't ought to be so jubilant perhaps he got already killed. God grant that he may come back safe home."

Who was diarist Hattie Pierce? Family documents indicate that she was born in Ohio in 1836 to parents Sidney and Hannah Hill Goodwin, who were originally from northern Vermont in the area around Lake Champlain. Her father was a builder who had gone west to pursue his trade along the route taken by the evolving railroads.

There is a family story that Sidney Goodwin went west to Indiana, leaving his wife and two young sons in Vermont with instructions to follow him in six months time unless she heard otherwise from him. Six months later, not having heard anything from her husband, Mrs. Goodwin—now considerably pregnant with Hattie—followed.

On a barge canal in Ohio, she left the little boys sleeping on the boat and stepped out to take a walk. She met her husband on the towpath walking in the other direction. His letter telling her to stay home had never been delivered.

Mr. Goodwin had not found sufficient work in Indiana to support a family and was on his way home when he met up with his wife. With all the household goods packed, the family home left behind, and his wife's approaching delivery, Mr. Goodwin set out for the home of relatives in Ohio where his daughter Hattie was born. Shortly thereafter, he returned to Indiana with his family and established a building business that followed the path of the railways as they moved west. Hattie grew up on the edge of what was then America's frontier. She obviously had some learning. She kept a diary, she wrote a great many letters, read books and periodicals and kept up with the political arguments of the day.

By the 1850s, the family lived in Terre Haute and kept a boarding house. Hattie's future husband Benjamin Franklin Pierce was one of the boarders. In 1857, he married her. Following the birth of their daughter, Eva, a year later, Pierce took Hattie back to Bradford, New Hampshire, to be closer to his aging parents and other family members.

When Franklin Pierce went off to war in 1862, he left Hattie in the home of his parents, Abigail and Nathan Pierce, on a neighboring farm in Bradford. She had three children, daughters Eva, Mamie, and Frankie. By January 1864, when this diary was started, Eva had recently died; Mamie was close to school age, and Frankie was a toddler. Hattie herself was not yet 30 years old.

Hattie's diary tells a story of a young mother and a housewife enmeshed in the daily life of children, housekeeping, in-laws, and neighbors—some friendly, some less so. Hers is also the story of an enterprising woman striving for a little financial independence, taking in sewing projects for the local mills and some private customers. During her husband's absence she also took on various projects related to the active operation of a farm—buying and selling animals, for example, and arranging for their slaughter and preservation. She writes of harvesting and preserving fruit, or of gathering food for dinner from one or another field.

In the middle of May of 1864, Hattie set out on a trip to Vermont, to visit her parent's relatives. For nearly two months, the diary records her visits among people, many of whom she had never before met. One entry notes, "I passed the house where my mother was born." Frankie, her littlest, accompanied her on this trip. Mamie stayed behind—again for reasons we don't know because they are not recorded.

Throughout the diary, Hattie records a constant refrain of care about her husband. Again and again she wonders: "Where is Frank? Is he safe? When will I hear from him again?" Her joy at hearing from him quickly gives way to renewed anxiety for his safety since writing the letter. She lived the year in the agony of not knowing; agony that in a sense was relieved in late October when she learned of his injury at the battle of Cedar Creek. Frank was injured, but he was spared death. A practical woman, Hattie settled for that fact.

I would like to conclude here with a word about style. To the best of my knowledge, Hattie Pierce never used a punctuation mark in her life. Her spelling is sometimes incorrect; her handwriting nearly illegible (though some of that is the effect of time on pencil lead), and punctuation is non-existent. To make this transcript more readable, I have added periods and an occasional question mark to separate sentences, and I have capitalized proper nouns when necessary. Otherwise, I have left spelling and odd turns of phrase as I found them.

S.C.

Hattie's 1864 diary

Jan. 1
All hail to a rainy new year. I am in hopes that my absent one will be home before another new year. My teeth ache today. Oh why dont I hear from Frank?

Jan. 2

This has been an afful cold day. I was going to have my teeth out but it was so cold. I could not go a nother day and no letter. What can be the matter. Mr. Hall and Hattie Sargent have been here today.

Jan. 3

Another cold day and no letter from Frank. I had two from home and had the tooth out today. G. Sargent came and staid with mother. I don't see why Frank don't write.

Jan. 4

It has been a cold day. I didn't dare walk for fear I would take cold in my teeth. I have made three pair of drawers. Frankie is quite unwell. No letter today.

Jan. 5

I was made glad today of one thing. A letter from my husband. I went to the corner to carry my drawers. It snowing all day. Frankie is quite unwell.

Jan. 6.

Len was here today. It was not very cold today. Frankie is better. I am making drawers. Oh my poor lonely soldier. I would give a good lot to see you.

Jan. 7

Not very cold today. I washed and washed floor. Sam was in in the evening. We look for Len he did not come. Oh I am so lonely without Frank.

Jan. 8

It has been a very cold day. Doctor Chesney been here and Len has been here to work. I rec two letters from my dear husban in the evening. Mr. Woodbury and his wife came in. All well.

Jan. 9

This has been a cold and windy day. I went to the upper village today. Woodbury rode home with me. I ironed after I came back. Father very lame. I don't know what've is.

Jan. 10

Not a very cold day. There has not been a soul in today except Frank Sargent. I am going to write to my dear husband. Tonight the wind blows.

Jan. 11

Monday. I washed today. Rather pleasant. I recd a letter from Frank an also sent one. I went to the village with Len. Frankie is not well tonight. I have made one pair of drawers tonight.

Jan. 12
Len has worked here today. I went over to Mrs. Woodburys and down to Mr. Cheney's. It has been a pleasant day. All well as usual.

Jan. 13
Been a pleasant day. Sargent and Len have worked here today. Ella Fitch G. S. wife and Hannah Sargent and Sam Hall have been in this evening 9 o.c. A letter from Frank tonight. I made two pair of drawers today.

Jan. 14
It has been a beautiful day. I have made four prs of drawers today. I must write to Frank tonight. Mrs. Woodbury and G. Sargant wife came in this evening. All well as usual.

Jan. 15
It snowed today. Len was here. I washed floors, ironed and made two pairs of drawers. G.S. came and brought Father a letter. It is pleasant tonight.

Jan. 16
It was windy this morning but clearing quite pleasant. I have made two pair of drawers today. Len brought a load of wood.

Jan. 17
It has been a pleasant day. Mother and Father were up to Lens. I got my allotment today. Sam has been in today.

Jan. 18
Monday. It has rained today. I have made two pair of drawers tonight. Len had the old [illegible] today. I hope I shall get a letter from Frank tomorrow.

Jan. 19
Tuesday. It has rained all day. I have made almost six pair of drawers. There has not been a person here today. Got up at half past eight. It is almost eleven.

Jan. 20
Wednesday. Quite cold and windy. I have been to the corner. I got 15 pairs of drawers. There has been no one here today. I expect to get a letter from Frank.

Jan. 21
This has been a beautiful day. I have made four pairs of drawers today. Len and Cintha have been here. I have been poping corn. I must write a little to Frank.

Jan. 22
This has been a beautiful day. Len came down this morning and brought me my much look for letter. I was made glad by knowing that my dear husband was well. I made five pairs of drawers today.

Jan. 23
This has been a pleasant day. I hear some news today. Maria Hall is married. Ella Fitch has been here today and Len has come in the evening. I have made but two pair of drawers today.

Jan. 24
Sunday. A pleasant day. Unkle Chapan and family have been here. Also Annee and Mattie and Addie. George Sargent brought me over a mess of fish.

Jan. 25
Monday. I have washed today and made one pair of drawers. Been quite pleasant but windy. Len finished loading wood today. I sent Berny a letter today.

Jan. 26
Tuesday. We have all been up to the village. I had Frankies picture taken. It has been verry windy today. I have made one pair of drawers tonight and eaten three apples. My I must write some to Frank.

Jan. 27
Been pleasant today. Mrs. Sargent been in this evening. Sam has been in. I rec a letter from cousin Jo tonight. I must write to Frank. I don't see why I don't get a letter back.

Jan. 28
Been beautiful day. I have been up to cors. I settled up my bill and also with [looks like Mess and Klen] I rec a letter from Frank tonight. Lib Gons is here tonight. I have paied out 20 dollars today.

Jan. 29
Pleasant day. Lib went home today. I went down and got Hannah Colins to come up to our house to stay with Mother. I am up to Lenards tonight. I am going up to Concord tomorrow.

Jan. 30
Not very pleasant today. I came down to C. found Mrs. Spaulding sick. Staid all night and had a good time. Spent $5,10cts.

Jan. 31
Sunday found me in Concord. It is rather stormy and unpleasant. I am going home tomorrow. I have been in all day. I feel anxious about the folks to home. I spent down to Concord $6,19cts.

Feb. 1
Finds me in Concord. I am going to start for home. It snows a perfect hurricane started and had a tooth out on the way. Came to Mr. Hams in the stage and he brought me home.

Feb. 2
Quite pleasant. Hanna Colins went up to Unkle Comens. Worked on baking all day. Got a letter from Frank yesterday. Dont feel very well.

Feb. 3
Verry plesant today. Went down to Ms. Cheneys to get some apples to send to Mrs. Spaulding. Got some. Paid a shiling for them.

Feb. 4
Quite cold. Went up to the depo to leave a box to go to Mrs. Spaulding. Sent a letter to Frank. Came home made some molasses candy corn and Unkle Comens was in.

Feb. 5
Been verry pleasant today. Cyntha been here. I washed the floors. Cut Mamie an apren. Father brought me ten pair of drawers to make. I have to t...ling tonight.

Feb. 6
Not very pleasant. I packed our apples today. X. I rec. two letters tonight. One from my dear husben and one from home. Made Mamie an apren.

Feb. 7
Sunday evening. Mrs. W. and George and his wife and Mr. Wheeler have been here this evening. Mr. Berly and his wife have been here today. Very pleasant today.

Feb. 8
Oh it is an afful blustry night. I have washed today and made one pair of drawers. Oh I should like to know where my poor soldier boy was tonight. I must write a little to him tonight.

Feb. 9
Been a cold day. Father has been in the house all day to work on our kandling. No soul has been here today. I have made the pairs of drawers today. Isled came tonight.

Feb. 10

It has been as cold as Greenland today. George Sergent has worked here today. I have made three pairs of drawers today and have beans for supper.

Feb. 11

Pretty cold day. Father went up to the corner. I finished my drawers today and read the paper tonight.

Feb. 12

Been verry pleasant today. I was made glad by getting a letter from my dear soldier boy. Sam and Charly Wheeler were in tonight.

Feb. 13

This has been a pleasant day. I washed the floors and find some combs. I wanted to go and hear mormon speak but was disappointed. I must write to my soldier boy. Father has gone to the lecture.

Feb. 14

Sunday. It has been a cold stormy day and oh the wind howls around. I have been reading all day and tonight G. General Nath S. Jil to Father. I finished my letter. Herbut and son have been in today.

Feb. 15

A pretty cold day. I went up to the Corner and got the box Frank sent and I also carried up my drawers 10 pairs. I washed in the forenoon. Mr. W. went with me.

Feb. 16

Oh but don't the wind blow tonight and the snow flies for it has snowed all day. I have not accomplished much today. I cut Maes dress lining out.

Feb. 17

This has been an afful day. The wind has blown a perfect hurrycane. There has not been a soul in today. I have not accomplished much today.

Feb. 18

Not quite so cold today. I have been riping up Franks old coat. Len has been here today. I weary today. Father has gone up to Unkles tonight.

Feb. 19

This has been a cold day. I went up to the corner. Met Cynth went up to the mills with. I sent a letter to Frank and I rec one from cousin Sarah. I have been reading Jonsen speech.

Feb. 20

This has been a pleasant day. Father went over to East Washington. Maria Anurid came down here. I rec a letter from My Darling Husban tonight. I might write some to him.

Feb. 21

Sunday. It has been pleasant day. Len and family have been here. Anna has been here and Is. I must write tonight.

Feb. 22

Not verry pleasant day. I washed today. Unkle Comens came in this evening. I have not accomplished much today. I must write to night.

Feb. 23

Been a beautiful day. I have had quite a tramp. Been up to Newbury with Cintha. I rec a letter from Frank tonight. God bless him. He is better than any other man.

Feb. 24

Quite pleasant day. There was some old straglers came in and wanted some breakfast. We gave them some. I worked on Mais dress. Father went up to the village.

Feb. 25

Been a beautiful day. I finished Mamie's dress and have been to work on a present for her birthday which is tomorrow. I send a letter tonight to Frank.

Feb. 26

Been a stormy day. Mr. Sargent has been here. I ironed today. Len came in. Mamies birthday. I have found out some things today.

Feb. 27

This has been quite a cold day. Father has been to an auctien. Sam and Charly Wheeler have been in here tonight. I have been reading but it is late.

Feb. 28

Sunday night. Mrs. and Grand Wife have been here tonight and also Len father have been here today. It has been quite a warm day.

Feb. 29

Quite pleasant day. I went up to the corner. I received a letter from Frank tonight and I must write some. Sugar. I not accomplished much today. I have thought a good deal of my dear Frank today for I dreamed of him last night.

Mar. 1
Pleasant day and a verry happy day for me. Frank came home. Mr. Cheney came in in the evening.

Mar. 2
Pleasant day. Len and family came down. G. S. and OCheny came in the evening and Unkle Comens. Frank went up to the corner.

Mar. 3
Cold and Windy. Frank has come to carry Cyntha home. Father been shelling corn. I have been baking and must go and iron.

Mar. 4
Pleasant day. I washed today. Mr. Woodbury and wife came in and spent the evening. Frank has an afful sore throat. Father went to mill today.

Mar. 5
A verry pleasant day. Father went and brought Aunt Esther home. Franks throat some better. Len worked here today. Frank and I went to a political meeting.

Mar. 6
Sunday rained all day. Frank and me going to ride but it rained so we could not. We have been in the house courting all day.

Mar. 7
Quite pleasant. Frank and I cleaned up the chamber. Franks throat comenced to feel sore and I looked down his throat and found he had the dyphera and we sent for a doctor.

Mar. 8
Frank is no better today. The doctor say he must not go to town meeting. He feels affuly. The doctor says it is dypthera. I feel worried about him. Cynth came down with folks.

Mar. 9
Cold and windy. Frank thinks he is a little better today. Mr. Hall came down to see Frank. The doctor came to see him today. Cyntha has gone home. We feel quite lonely.

Mar. 10
Been a pleasant day. Frank is a little better today. Mr. Woodbury and wife came in a few minutes in the evening. Mr. Wheeler and Herbut came in also. I am in hopes Frank is going to get a long nicely now.

Mar. 11
A stormy day. It rains hard. The doctor has been here. He says Frank is doing well. Doctor Cheney came in to see Frank and also Mr. Hall in the evening.

Mar. 12
A beautiful day. Baked some today. Frank is still on the gain. Doctor says he wont be able to go for some time. Cyntha came down today.

Mar. 13
A stormy day. Frank is still gaining. Woodbury and wife came in and also Mr. Baily and a soldier friend of Franks. It has been a very unhappy day to me.

May. 14
Cold and windy. I washed today. Frank is still better. Sam is in here this eveing. I am pretty tired tonight. I have not accomplished much today.

Mar. 15
Pleasant day. Been up to the village. Frank is better. I have not done much work today. Been getting my cloth ready to make my saque.

Mar. 16
Cold and windy. Mr. Cressy and Mr. Fitch have been in today. I have baked some and cleaned some today.

Mar. 17
Been pleasant day. I went to the village today. Frank went as far as Mr. Wheelers with me. The reg has gone.

Mar. 18
Been cold and windy. Mr. Fitch has been here today to work. Mr. G. Sergent has been up tonight. It is cold as Greenland. I must snugup to Frank.

Mar. 19
Cold and squaly, Frank and I went to the Village. Frank got his firlough extend ten days longer. Mr. Fitch worked here today.

Mar. 20
Cold day had a company all day. Len Faith and Herbut folks and Unkle Chapen. I have been reading today.

Mar. 21
Cold and windy. I washed today. Dear Frank is here with me and I am happy. Went to Mr. Fitchs in the evening.

Mar. 22
Pleasant day. Worked on my saque today. Went to Mr. Wheelers tonight. Not accomplishing much today.

Mar. 23
Pleasant day but oh my dear Frank has got to go off. He went to the village to see the doctor today. I ironed and finished my saque today.

Mar. 24
Cold and windy. Went to Mr. A. Pokershals and got my money. Went to Lens and staid all night. Oh dear my darling has got to go off.

Mar. 25
Beautiful day. We Frank and I went to Concord and it has been one of the saddest days of my life. I had to part with my dearest husban. Oh God bless and protect him shall be my earnest prayer.

Mar. 26
Another pleasant day but I miss my dear Frank so I get so lonely. I can't stay here nothing. Evening find me at home but oh it is so lonely. I miss the well known home.

Mar. 27
Pleasant day but oh such a lonely one to me. Frances has been here today and Cynth. Oh if I only knew where my dear Frank was.

Mar. 28
Pleasant day. I washed today and mended some.

Mar. 29
Beautiful day. I went to the village and what is more pleasant I got a letter from my dear husban. Oh I wish I knew where he was tonight. Lib Jones has been here today.

Mar. 30
Cold stormy day. I ironed today. Sam Hall was in today. Mr. Moss came then Mr. Manning and we all singned.

Mar. 31
It stormed all day. I have been busy sewing all day. Sam Hall came in a few minutes. Nothing of importance happened today.

April 1
A rainy day. I went to carry Aunt Esther home. We did not meet with a verry warm reception. I was most starved when I got home. We lost the way twice.

April 2
An afful stormy night and it has stormed all day. There has not been any one oh yes Len was here today. I have been puttering all day. Wrote to Jenny Spaulding tonight.

April 3
Pleasant day. Hattie Sargent has been over here today; Herberts in this eve. I have been so lonely today. I don't know to do. I wish I knew where Frank was.

April 4
Beautiful day. Len sent for me to come up and see to Cyntha. She is sick with sore throat. I went and also up to the doctor and to see about getting my dress fitted.

April 5
Cold and cloudy. I have been to have my dress fitted today and I walked up to the mills and am afful tired.

April 6
Pleasant day. Cut out a Lora Wheeler saque. Mr. Fitch came up and got some work to do for me. Father bought a waggon today.

April 7
Pleasant day. I went to the village in the morning. Len and George Doulng came in here. I worked on my new dress.

April 8
Pleasant day. I washed floors the forenoon. Went to Aunt Carolines to get some milk this afternoon.

April 9
Pleasant day. I went to the village to see about the flower. Mr. Barly sent it for me. Ellen went with me. I wanted to hear from my Dear Frank but oh I did not get a letter.

April 10
It has stormed all day hard. I went down to see how Mrs. Cheny was getting along. There has not been a living soul oh yes Herbet was in this morning.

April 11
It has snowed all day. The snow is over a foot deep. Father went to the village and got the flower. I have been sewing all day.

April 12
It has snowed some today. The snow is over a foot deep. I have heard from my Dear husban tonight. Oh I am so thankful that he is still alive.

April 13
Stormed part of the day. I went to the village and took dinner with Cynth. I sent a letter to Frank. Finished off my drawer in the afternoon.

April 14
Stormed when I got up but cleared off. I washed and have been sewing on Mamies dress. I am almost sick tonight.

April 15
Pleasant day. Mother and Aunt went visiting up to Unkles. I ironed in the forenoon baked some flapjacks for supper.

April 16
Pleasant day. Mrs. J. S. came over here today. I washed the floors in the forenoon. I recd a letter from Jenny today. I finished Mamies dress tonight.

April 17
Stormy and sunshine. Mr. Hall came in told me there was a letter from Frank. I do wish I could get it. I went up to Unkles and bought some bulls.

April 18
Cold day. I washed in the forenoon. Went up to the depo expecting to meet Mrs. Spaulding but she did not come. I rec a letter from my dear tonight.

April 19
This has been a stormy day. I have finished my dress today. Olive Mansfield has been here today and is here tonight. It looks as though it would be pleasant tomorrow.

April 20
Quite pleasant today. I have been making a waist for Mamie to wear. Jeticklos has been here today. I have written to Frank tonight.

April 21
It has been a beautiful day I have been sick today. I have not accomplished much

today. There has been a number in two day. Doctor Cheny among the rest.

April 22
I have been sick toay not verry pleasant today oh do wish I could feel well for I have so much to do.

April 23
It has been a beautiful day but I don't feel as though I could enjoy myself very well for I am so unwell I have not done much today.

April 24
This has been a pleasant day. I feel some better today. I went visit Dear Little Eva grave. Oh my dear lost darling.

April 25
It has been a cloudy day. I did not feel well enough to wash today.

April 26
It has been a cloudy day. I washing this morning and went up to the village this afternoon. It rains tonight.

April 27
Cloudy and rainy. I have been sewing all day. Mr. P. Sargent came over to tell Father he could not come and help him.

April 28
Been pleasant day. I have been going to went up to the depo. Jenny Spaulding came up. I rec a letter from my dear soldier tonight.

April 29
Not verry pleasant day. Jenny and I went up to the village and carried up some eggs to the depo.

April 30
This has been a pleasant day. I find myself in Concord and just as tired as I can be. I do wish I knew where Frank was.

May 1, 1864
Not verry pleasant day. I have been sewing all day. Went for a walk in the evening. The first of May finds me at Concord.

May 2
Beautiful day. I have not done much today. Been on the trot. Had Mamie hair cut.

May is not well tonight. I am going to start for Bradford tomorrow.

May 3
Cold and rainy in the forenoon. I came home today left my little Mamie. I rec a letter from my Dear husban and also one from home. I feel tired. I walked home from the depo.

May 4
This has been a beautiful day. Mother birthday. I wish I had something to give her. Mrs. Sargent came over and brought me a letter from my dear soldier. I have been writing to him.

May 5
This has been a beautiful day. I have been a calling today. I eat dinner to Mrs. Ganes. I have been hunting bulls for Mrs. Spaulding. I have finished my letter. I am tired so I don't know what to do.

May 6
This has been the warmest day of the season. Len raise up his house today. I went to the corner today. Cynth came down to our house today.

May 7
A cloudy day. I went to the village this afternoon and I am tired almost to death. I have not accomplished much today.

May 8
This has been rather unpleasant day. I went up to Unkles to see Herbut.

May 9
Been a pleasant day. I have washed today. Doctor Cheny came in today. I am afful tired tonight.

May 10
Windy. Home until evening. I went down to Mr. Chenys. Doctor gave me some aples. Wrote to cousin Jo.

May 11
Wendsdy. Rained today. I have been sewing today.

May 12
Not verry pleasant day. Cleaned the front room. Went to the village in the afternoon. Anna Peerce was here, also Ella.

May 13
Misty day. Been sewing all day. No one has been here today. I hope it will clear off.

May 14
Cloudy. Went to the village. Had two teeth out. Got the children hats. Rec two letters one from my dear husban and one from home. To supper at Mr. Fitchs.

May 15
Rained all day. There has not been a living soul in today. I have sewed some, read some and wrote some.

May 16
Cloudy and rainy. I went to the village had two teeth out rec. three dollars from A. A. Marshall.

May 17
Pleasant day. Oh we had a thunder shower in the afternoon. Went up to dear little Evas grave also to Aunt Carolines. Aunt was down here this evening.

May 18
Pleasant day and it finds me at Concord with my little ones. Oh my teeth do feel so bad. I expect to start for Vt. in the morning.

May 19
This night finds me at Vermont. I had a verry nice ride on the cars. It has been a beautiful day. I think I shall like first rate. Frankie is very good.

May 20
Pleasant day here. I am away up at Vt. and like the folks verry much. Went up to the depo to meet cousin Joseph. Rec a letter from my darling.

May 21
Pleasant in the forenoon. Came over to Westford today. Like the folks verry much indeed. Came past the place where my mother was born.

May 22
Pretty cold but still at Westford Sunday and it is pretty still here. I like verry much indeed. I see Aunt Fanny and I think she is good.

May 23
Not verry pleasant day. I find myself at Westford. I wrote three letters today. Maria went home today.

May 24
Rainy day. Have not accomplished much today.

May 25
Rainy day. Nothing of importance today. I am likening here very well.

May 26
Pleasant day and Frankies birthday. I am still at Westford. I like very much.

May 27
Not verry pleasant. Went over to Aunt Betsy Rogers a visiting. Had a verry nice visit.

May 28
Been a pleasant day. Nothing of importance today.

May 29
Sunday quite cool today. Went for a walk, sent Frank a letter. I don't see why I don't get a letter.

May 30
A beautiful day. I am having a nice visit. I washed some today.

May 31
Not verry pleasant day. Rode out. Went to Westford Center. Enjoyed the ride verry much.
[What follows is an entry that appears to have been recorded later. It looks like an August entry, in fact.]

August [looks like 2].
I washed and laid down to rest my weery bones and did not chang my dress until I was caught Dr. Cheny came in and I skadded upstairs to change my apparel. I was mortified for there was my legs plane to be seen. I have finished Aunties dress. Oh dear I have forgot my emptiness. Oh how provoking.

June 1, 1864
It is cloudy and rains some. I expect to go away today. Went to Georgia today. Came back to my cousin. Dont feel half so much at home. I am ever so homesick tonight.

June 2
Rather cool in the morning. We had a thunder shower in the afternoon. I don't feel quite so homesick today but don't like here so well as I did to Cousin Sarah.

June 3

Went to Mrs Sibleys my cousin and say the only unkle I have and cousin Irene. Unkle brought me to Georgia. I am glad to get back.

June 4

Pleasant day. I have felt tired today but I like here very much. I do hope cousin Jo will come home. He has come home. Oh I heared from my Deer Husband.

June 5

Not very pleasant day. We went up on the Hill to get wintergreen. I do like cousin Jo first rate. I enjoy myself first rate.

June 6

This has not been very pleasant day. I have been to work on a apern for Frankie. I have written two letters. Cousin is going away in the morning. I am sorry.

June 7

Very cold and wind for this time of the year. I went to see Mrs. Loughren this afternoon. I have been sewing on Frankies apren.

June 8

Went to visit and old friend of my mothers. Had a verry nice visit. Rather a cold day. I was disappointed I did not get a letter.

June 9

It has rained all day today. I wrote some to Frank. I rec a letter from Cinth today. Oh dear I did not get a letter tonight.

June 10

Cold day. Been reading Darkness and day light. Not accomplished much today. Sewing Frankies apren. Been a rainy day. Oh dear why don't I get a letter.

June 11

Cold and windy. I find myself at my only unkles. Like him and cousin Irene very much. Think I shall have a very good visit. Frankies rather cross today.

June 12

This is the Lords day. It has been quite pleasant today I attended devine services this morning. Came home and wrote to Len. Rec a letter from Len two days ago.

June 13

Pleasant day. Cay and I have been washing today. Did not hurry much. Did not think it worth while. Went to Mrs. Sibley in the evening.

June 14
Very pleasant day. We put our clothes out this morning. I am to work on my morning dress. Oh dear why don't I get a letter from my Deer husban.

June 15
Not been doing much today. Been very pleasant day Rode out in the eveing with Mrs. Wheelock. Got some more cloth for my dress.

[The following entry is recorded on the pages for June 16, 17 & 18. However, I believe it was recorded later:]

July fourth finds me at Mr. Brigs in Vt. I have not been to any selebration but think I have enjoyed myself as well. I have read dear Franks letters and wrote to him. but if I could only see him I should like it much better. Oh I do hope he is well tonight. But it is late and I must go to bed. There has been considerable going on tonight.

[No entry for June 18th.]

June 19
Been an afful hot day today. We thought we would not go to church to day. Irene and Cad down to Georgia. I rec three letters. One from my deer husban, two I mean.

June 20
Not quite so warm today. We washed this morning. Riped our hats of in the afternoon and carried them to the miliner. [They took the trimming off hats and took them to be retrimmed.]

June 21
Very warm today. Ironed some in the morning. Went up Mrs. Elle Clemens in the afternoon. Bell Hendrick came up. She brought my hat home.

June 22
Had a verry pleasant visit. Went to Mrs. Crowns Walked up and had a splendid ride back. Wrote to mother. Cousin Jo came in in the evening I do wish I could know my Deer was well tonight.

June 23
Very warm today Mrs. O. had sent for us to come by there and go strawberrying. Went but did not get many but have pretty good time. Staid to supp. Had some compliments.

131

June 24

Very warm. I washed out some things in the morning. We went down street in the evening. Quite cold when we got home.

June 25

An afful hot day this has been. I ironed this morning. We had an invitation to go to the show and went and found it quite interesting but not so much so. Oh I did a letter from my Dear husban. Oh I do love to hear from him.

June 26

This has been another warm day but looks like rain. I came over to East Georgia to thinking to go to Cambrige I hope I shall get a chance to go.

June 27

Verry cold today. Old Mr. Butts did not come. I am afraid he wont. I am real disappointed. I most wish I have staid to Milton.

June 28

Not very warm today I begin to think I am not agoing to have a chance to go to Cambrige. I went away to dinner today. I had a chat with Mr McEllan this evening.

June 29

Quite pleasant day I guess I shant forget it soon. I rode to Cambridge today and oh such a ride. I broke my perisol and I almost spoiled my shall and I wish I had staid where I was.

June 30

Quite pleasant day. I don't think I like to stay here very well. I feel pretty homesick but I suffer it because I have to put on my dignity. Oh I wish I was with Frank but this can't be.

July 1, 1864

Quite pleasant day. Cousin Sarah and I rode out today. When we came home we found Aunt Lucy. I was verry glad to see her.

July 2

Oh dear, I have been afful home sick to day. I expected to go home today but it has rained all day steady. I shall be glad when I get home.

July 3

Oh dear what a lone some day. I went to church this morning but Frankie was so naughty I could not stay. Went again this afternoon.

July 4

This has been a day long to be remembered for it is the coldest fourth of July I ever witnessed I came from Cambrige today. I rec three letters from Frank. One had two dollars in it.

July 5

Quite pleasant. Took a little ride on the cars. Came from Georgia to Milton. I guess I am glad to get back to Renes again. Oh feel quite to home here Laura came down with me.

July 6

I have been washing today. It rained this morning but has been quite pleasant this afternoon. Cay and I went for a walk. I rec a letter from Ella tonight.

July 7

Been a beautiful day. Went to Mrs. Sibley a visiting. Had a very nice visit. Frankie has been quite good.

July 8

I ironed some today. Been quite pleasant today. Rene and I have staid home today. I have been to work on my waist and oh on Maimies dress.

July 9

Not accomplished much today. Had a nice ride. Came up to Amanda Crowns tonight. I think I shall like first rate.

July 10

Sunday morning finds me at cousin Amandas. A beautiful place I like verry much. Heard that poor Sarah Rogers was dead. I am very sorry for her poor mother.

July 11

Quite pleasant in the morning. I washed some today. Cuz A and I went to the falls. I am afraid I got cold. I was in hopes to have heard from my dear Frank.

July 12

Woke up with an afful sore throat but went to Sarah Rogers furnel. I feel afful bad tonight. I am afraid I am going to be sick.

July 13

Was afful sick last night and have been all day. I have an attack of dythera but took a sweat and I guess I will remember it for a long time. We had such a laugh.

July 14
I feel much better today but don't feel near well yet. Oh Dear I do want to hear from Frank. I don't see why I don't get a letter.

July 15
I am still getting better. I do like the Crown girls. Amanda is such a good girl and so is Liddy. Oh if I could only hear from Frank.

July 16
I feel pretty well today. I am glad I was here when I was sick. Frankie likes to stay here. I rec a letter from Len Spaulding today.

July 17
This has been a beautiful day. Cuz A and I went down to Renes. Had a nice ride. Came home and had a real laugh at Frankie. I do want to hear from Frank.

July 18
We washed today. Henry Rogers wanted me to go over there but I can't yet a while. I do want a letter from Frank I dont know [page runs out at this point]

July 19
I have been visiting. I find myself at cousin Albans. They are pretty nicely fixed. I wonder what I will dream. I hope it will be something good about my Dear Frank.

July 20
Oh I am quite in good spirits. I have five letters from my husband. I am so glad to hear from him once more but I dont know where he is now. Oh I wish I did.

July 21
This has been a cold day. I came up to Amandas today. I feel quite to home tonight. I have been fixing my dress so Mrs. Crown has been here making her dress to day.

July 22
An afful cold day. Cousin Sarah came a long this morning and wanted me to go avisiting with her. I am going home with her and tonight finds me at Westfield. I like first rate.

July 23
Saturday. Not verry pleasant looking in the morning but cleared off and has been quite pleasant after all. I have not accomplished much today.

July 24
Sunday. I have read a little and slept a little and sewing a little and eat a good dinner

and that is about all I have done. I do wish I knew where F is.

July 25
I have been to Milton today. Had a very nice visit. Cousin Sarah went to a furnel to day. We had to come home in the rain. I paied 25 cts for cotten today 10 for paper.

July 26 [continues into the 27th]
Rained in the morning. Sarah went to a nother furnel today and I staid at home. It clerd off. Sarah came home and a good lot of hurry blurry here. I guess I am glad I have two letters from Frank. I cant say that I am very glad he is on the Potomac but I was so anxious to know where he was. Oh dear would I be glad when this war is over.

July 28
Not very pleasant day. Still at Westfield not doing anything of importance.

July 29
Pleasant day. Mrs Prat and Emma have been here today. Like them verry much. Rec a letter from Concord. Was so disappointed because it was not from Bradford.

July 30
A verry pleasant day. Jo and Marie have been here today. Jo brought me a letter from Frank. Oh dear I was so sorry to see Petersburg in it but guess we can't have every thing we want in this world.

July 31
A very warm day. Packed up to go to Milton today. Hen and Sarah came over with me. Went up to Georgia had a friend of two pedls. Pretty good time but afful warm. Mailed two letters today. Came back to Milton and stoped to Rene and oh horror I forgot to take all my things out. Dear me I am so sorry for I wanted to work some and there is no use crying for spiled milk so I might as well take it cool.

Aug. 1, 1864
Well a nother month comenced and finds me still at Vt but my sojurn here is almost over. It is hot enough to kill today. I been visiting to Milton. Got caught in a shower but dont care if it will cool the air.

Aug. 2
Woke up this morning found it raining. I hope it will cool the air. I was going visiting but I will have to stay in doors to day. Been working on my dress.

Aug. 3
Rains this morning but has cleared off. Been packing up all the morning. Tonight

finds me at Mrs. George Ashley all ready for an early start in the morning.

Aug. 4
Well I have got started for the old granite, and not a verry pleasant day. Well I have got to Concord after jolting all day and being about all over Concord.

Aug. 5
Hurrugh for home. I hope to see there this afternoon and here I am. Well there is no place like home after all. I have a letter waiting me and I guess I was glad. Well I must off for bed. Oh I am so glad to get to my little darling Mamie.

Aug. 6
Oh so tired as I have been today I have hardly stired out the house and I don't feel as though I could. I believe it has been pleasant.

Aug. 7
Oh dear there is Andrew Jones and family. No rest for the wicked. I wish my body could rest. Sunday it has been nothing but company all day. I sent my soldier a letter. I found time for that but it was as much as ever.

Aug. 8
All hail to wash day I suppose somebody would say but I can't see if rub dub dub all day. Oh Dear I am glad it don't come any oftener. I have written to Rene to night.

Aug. 9
Well a nother day is gone. The birthday of my lost Eva my precious angel. I little thought on her last birthday that it would be the last. Oh my Eva little Eva.

Aug. 10 and into 11
Well another day has gone. I began the morning by going to the Village. Came home read my Franks letters to Mother and Aunt. Ironed. Eat my dinner. Read some in the ledger. Wrote to Frank and loaded two loads of hay and I think it has been a day of usefullness.

Aug. 11
Well I am so tired to night. I ironed and went a berrying and had company and to night Sam has been in and I could not write as I intended to.

Aug. 12
Verry warm day. I went to the village. Spent 3 34ct. I sent some things to my Dear Frank. Oh Dear how lonely it is to be a grass widdow and I must go to bed a lone.

Aug. 13

A nother hot morning here. It is almost seven and I am just out of bed. Not a very good beginning for a great days events. Well I have accomplished a good lot today more than I can write down tonight.

Aug. 14

The Sabath. Pleasant day. I attended divine service down to the Pond. I got so hungry that I had to come home. I don't believe that I will take another such a tramp soon.

Aug. 15

I am so afful tired tonight poor dierie that I cant stay talking long with washing and getting hay and everything. Oh I dont feel as though I could get to bed.

Aug. 16

I have not accomplished much to day but I am so tired.

Aug. 17

Woke up and found it rainy. I am glad of it to be true. I do love to hear it rain. I went up stairs and laid down and heard it rain. I rec a letter from my dear Frank.

Aug. 18

Cleared off beautiful. I went padling around the ground to get some thing for a boiled dish. I succeeded in getting a few beets in 88.

Aug. 19

Oh dear there comes old Aunt Lee so I thought today but poor old soul how tired she looks. Well I went and carried her home. Went down to Mrs. Frichs and did not get home until after dark.

Aug. 20

I expected it was going to rain this morning but Ella and started any way. Went to Mr Gilmores. Had a pleasant visit but he's not got many blackberries. We did not get home until 8.

Aug. 21 [the following entries are nearly illegible]

Well another Sabbeth has come and almost gone. I washed the children a work I usually do Saturday night. I went to bed and had a fine sleep and carried Cynt h home. Oh dear here [page ends]

Aug. 22

Well another Monday has come and is almost gone. I think how much nearer Frank's time is already gone. Rub a dub on Monday. Oh dear I am glad wash day is over but I must stop and give up my remeniscing.

Aug. 23
Tuesday has been a pretty busy day with me. I expected I would go to make Aunt Lee dress but I found so much to that I staid at home airing my clothes and went to Mrs. Whitcombs in the afternoon. Had a good visit.

Aug 24
Pleasant day. Went over and fitted Aunt Lee dress. I crossed the brook on a pole. I have had the headache all day. What a lot of folks went to the caravan.

Aug. 25
Oh dear I do feel dreadful bad today. Took some medics was unfit for duty in the forenoon. Oh am I glad I have rec a letter from my dear soldier. Oh I am so sorry he has had to go into the field.

Aug. 26
I have worked real hard to day washed the floor and helped to fill a bed and cleaned up the other room and I must finish my letter to my dear soldier boy. Oh dont I wish I could see him tonight.

Aug. 27
I have been up to the Village today. I rec 16 dollars and spent 8.66 cts. Doing pretty well I think. Oh Dear what lots of money it does cost to get any thing with.

Aug. 28 through 30
Another Sunday come and gone or almost gone. It has been a beautiful day. I went to my dear little Eva grave. Blessed angel. Oh may it please the all omnipotence to spare my little one and oh may I meet my little Eva in heaven. How lonely I do feel this time of the year. I wonder why it is that I always do feel so lonely in the fall. Oh my precious husband how I long for your dear society. Cynth and family have been here today. [30] Sunday I trespassed on the day but I must write my thoughts. Father had a cousin a stranger call on him today.

Aug. 31
Oh Dear what a cold day. I have been froze all day. I went to the corner and I rec a letter from my Dear Frank. I spent 49 cts an rec 60 for making old sun dress
[further down]
End of August I guess. I will have occasion to remember it for a long time. I never did hear any one take on as old Aunt Caroline. Oh how afful it must be for any one to have such a disposition. I had to take out her sleeves and I do declare I hope I dont have to spend another afternoon there soon.

Sept. 1 running into 2
Well this day has passed away and old Perce Sargent lived through it. Mrs. Tiel took dinner here today and old Perce has been packing the barn. I have not done much sewing today. I am just as tired as the dog tonight such a tramp as I have had. I have been to Mrs. Jones. Met around he the corner and I am glad that I have got that bill straitened up any way.

Sept. 3
This has not been so pleasant a day as I wish it had been for it is the anniversary of my wedding. Oh where is poor Frank I wonder. 9 years have passed on wings it seems to me.

Sept. 4 running into 5
I have hear rumors of to my precious soldier to night. Father and I went to the firnel of Mr. Newton Cheeny. Poor soldier was not permitted to see Friends and home but Gods way is not our way. It rains slowly to night enuf to give any one the blues.

Sept. 5
Tuesday I went to Cynth this afternoon and took both children. I paid 45 cts for meat. 15 to Cynth. It was dark when I got home. Sam spent the evening with us.

Sept. 6
I am so tired I don't know what to do so I wont do anything. I spent 25 cts today.

Sept. 7
Been a beautiful day. I washed today rather late in the week but better late than never. Mother and Aunt went to make Aunt Sucky a visit. Had a good time they said.

Sept. 8 and 9
Oh dear how tired I am and my tooth aches affuly and Frankie seemed to be sick. I have been the longest tramp today. We went away down to Sutton. I thought of my precious husband. We went the same road four years ago. Oh I would that he was here now tonight. I feel so I dont know how.

Sept. 10
Quite a pleasant day. Thought I would go to the village to see if there would be something from my precious husban but Father went and oh me no letter. Why dont I get a letter?

Sept. 11
This has been a long and lonely day. Oh I do miss the dear companionship of my darling Frank. I thought this evening what I would give to see my dearest husband.

What evening is there but I think of him?

Sept. 12
Sunday Sept the 18 been at home all day. Not a living soul here to day. Oh how lonely I have been. I had a frency. Well I will have to pay for it.

Sept. 13
Oh what a lonely day. I have the blues so to night I dont know what to do. Oh father says that Captain Chandler is dead. Oh I do hope and pray it is not so. I was in hopes to have gone up to see if there was a letter from Frank.

Sept 14
It has been an afful lonely day. I was so disappointed. I went up to the village on purpose to get a letter and there wasnt any.

Sept. 15
Oh why dont I hear from my beloved husband? I walked up to the village this afternoon on purpose to get a letter and oh dear I did not find it.

Sept. 16
Quite an adventorius day. Mr. Whitcomb and I went to Newport. Had a nice time but oh horrors I guess it was not very nice having 8 teeth out. Ugh but didn't it hurt.

Sept 17 and 18
Couldn't sleep last night. I dont know wether it was drinking so much whiskey or the effect of having so many teeth out. I did think I should be glad when home arrived. We had a very pleasant time coming home. I do hope Mrs. Whitcomb wont get sick. I must to bed am so sleepy. Oh hope I shall dream of my precious husban.

Sept. 19
Not accomplished much to day. Went to see how Ira Sargent was this morning. Found he was very sick. Came home ironed a little. Eat so much hominy that I had to go to bed had quite sick.

Sept 20
Quite a busy day. Went and carried Cinths home an found a letter from my dear Frank. I feel amply paid my time for going to the village. I got tidings from my precious husban. Father and I went to the performance in the evening.

Sept 21
Willy Sears has been here to day. Oh deer I am so anxious about Frank to night.

Sept. 22
Did not accomplish much to day. Oh dear I am so worried about Frank. Oh God grant that he's spaired. Cinth is down here but she could offer no consolation.

Sept 23
I have been to the village to day. I waited thinking perhaps I should hear something from Frank but there was no account of him. Oh dear how anxious I am. I rec twelve dollars to day.

Sept. 24
Oh I do hope Frank has been spaired. I cant tell how anxious I do feel about my precious husban.

Sept. 25
Oh this has been an afful lonely day. I have been thinking where is my poor Frank. Oh I am afraid that some thing has befallen him. I went over to see how Ira was. He was better.

Sept. 26
This has been a cold raw day. I washed went to the village to see if I could hear any thing from my precious husban. No tidings. I paid Mr. Cressy 75 cts. Paid 72 at the store.

Sept. 27
Well Cynth and I been fixing up the home. Mother and Father have gone to E. Washington. Oh I was so glad. I heard from dear old Frank. Oh we feel lonely tonight.

Sept. 28 and 29 [run together on one page]
Well I came pretty near staying away from home. I thought Mother and Father was going to stay over to Washington all night but they came home and I guess I was glad. I did not want to stay to Mr Halls and I didnt mean to if I staid all alone. [Sept. 30] Oh what a hard time the 14 have had poor fellows. What a sore fate they have met with. Such a long list of killed and wounded.

Sept. 30
Oh it is cold and gloomy tonight. It rained all the morning. Oh I was disappointed in not getting a letter from my precious husban. Oh I am afraid that something has befallen him.

Oct. 1
Pleasant day. I baked in the forenoon. Went up to the village in the afternoon to get some tidings of my precious husban but no letter. Oh dear why dont I hear?

Oct. 2

It has rained steady all day. Oh it has been a afful lonely day. Not a living soul but Len here today. Oh I wonder where my Frank is tonight.

Oct. 3

Not very pleasant day. Washed and made jelly in the afternoon. Tired after day. My hands all stained so I cant sew.

Oct. 4

Beautiful day. Lib Jones has been here today. I have not accomplished today. Went down and helped Lib over the brook. We was a most afraid to we should tumble in.

Oct. 5

This has been a splendid day. I have been to work on my wash basket and I went to the village this afternoon to see if I should get a letter from my dear Frank but no letter. Oh dear I hope he is well.

[No record for Oct. 6. Oct. 7 — a long passage that covers space for 7-9, and is dated:]

Oct. 10.

Have not room enough to write all I have been doing since I had a chat with my dear friend. Carrie Peasly has been here. Went up to the village and called to Mr. Choatts and waited for the mail and oh I guess I was paid for waiting. I had a letter from my Dear Frank. I have been making me a wash basket and I wrote the letter the 9 and today I have been climbing trees and gathering apples and I am just as tired as I can be. Oh I was in hopes to have gone up to the village to see if there was a letter.

Oct. 10

How do you do poor neglected diary and my fast friend? I have had company and I have had something els to since I have had a chat with you and that is a letter from my Dear Frank and he is well oh and that good news.

Oct. 11

Oh dear I am tired tonight and it is cold and gloomy I have been busy today I went to the village but no letter. Oh dear why dont I hear from my dear Frank?

Oct. 12

Quite pleasant. I washed this forenoon and went to Mill this afternoon. Ella went with me. We went to Mrs Halls. Had a very pleasant chat.

Oct. 13

Oh Deer what a dreery day I did think this morning I could not wait until night to see the paper but it rained so Father thought he could not go. Oh dear how I do want to hear from my precious Frank. Oh what if he's wounded and suffering from the want of care? Oh I cant bear the thought.

Oct. 14

Oh how thankful I am tonight. I have heard from my precious husban. Oh I thank the heavenly Father for spairing my husband through so many dangers.

Oct. 15

This has been a very cold unpleasant day. I have been puttering. Have not accomplished much. I am going to wright a letter to my darling.

Oct. 16

Rather a cloudy day. I attended Mrs. Stanleys furnel today. One more friend gone to her last resting place. Mr. Stanly called to see me. Oh I am so glad to see any one so near home. He says he sees a victory day. I must go down to Mrs. Cressy and see him.
[The following passage falls on Oct. 17 through 20.]

Oct. 21

Dear Diary I have shamefully neglected you. I will try to inform what I have been doing all this time. I went to Mrs. Cressys on Monday afternoon it being a very pleasant day. Tuesday I was home all day until towards night. I went up to the office and I rec a letter from my Dear Frank. Oh I am so glad to hear from my dear husban. I went up to Lens Wendesday night and I had to get some tea and oil which was 60 cts. I rec 10 dollars from dear Frank in my letter. I went again last night and rec a nother letter. Oh how good my dear Frank is. He sent me 250 in the other letter.

Oct. 21

Mr Stanly called in to see me. He is going away to morrow. I have been to Mrs. Fritchs today. Had a very splendid visit so good night dear Diary.

Oct. 22

It has been a beautiful day. I baked this morning and went to the village this afternoon. I bought the children some shoes and I got half pound of tea and tobacco. Mr Stanly went away this morning.

Oct. 23 - 25

This has been a beautiful day. I and Aunt have improved some. Have been so rotten again. Had a very good dinner at Mrs. Frillbrooks. Met with rather a more pleasant reception this time. Oh I do wish I knew where the being most dear to me is. Alas

I know not whether he is on the land of the living or not. Oh when will this cruel war end so our much beloved ones will be home? Alas who knows the heart ache of the poor soldier wife and who can tell the suffering of that poor soldier no one but those that have experienced.

Oct. 26
At home all day. Went down to the crossing and got the daily but no thing in it about the old 14. Oh dear Frank I would give all the world to know that you was well tonight.

[No entry for Oct. 27.]

Oct. 28
Oh this has been an afful rainy day. I have hear sad news indeed from my soldier. I have hear he is wounded. Dear Frank I do hope that you dont suffer much but I am so thankfull he is spared that I cant feel so bad about his wound.

Oct. 29
Not very pleasant day. Been to the village. Rec twelve dollars. Sent two to Frank. Spent 1.10 cts. The Copperheads had a powwow. Oh dearst how I would like to share your pain if you could only be here tonight.

Oct. 30
How do you do my old Friend I have been neglecting of late and I consider an apoligy. This is Sunday evening Nov. 6

Oct. 31
My dear husban come home Nov. the 8 and I have had company and I don 't know what all I have been doing but I will try on the proceeding pages to acct. I have been quite busy today baked pumpkin pies. Finished writing a letter to my Dear Frank. Send it up by Cintha. My precious little Eva was here this time last year and the times fast drawing near that her precious spirit took its flight. Oh my precious Eva how sorry mama is for all her unkindness to you. Lord help me to do right by my other precious little ones.

Nov. 1, 1864
Not pleasant at all but yet it has been a day with surprise and pleasure for me. I went over to Mr Sargent and when I came home I found my Frank. I am so glad he has arrived safe.

Nov. 2
I went to the village today. Carried Cinth home. Bought Frank a neck tie 68 cts sugar 50 oil 30. I did not get home until dark.

Nov. 3

Quite pleasant today. Carrie Peesly came over to see Frank. I was glad to see Carrie as I am always.

Nov. 4

Oh what a rainy morning. Carrie will not go home today I dont believe. Rained all day as hard as it could pour. Len and Andrew Jones came in and eat their dinner.

Nov. 5

Cold as greenland this morning. Went to the village with Carrie. Oh what a time we had. Oh I never got home until one c'clock. I guess my Frank was lonely.

Nov. 6

Pleasant and cold. I am so glad that Frank is to home these cold stormy days. I don't think his foot is any better.

Nov. 7

Cold raw day. Washed this morning. Went to the village in the afternoon. Bought some oysters and tea and spices. The Union folks had a flag raising. Not a very large crowd out.

Nov. 8

This is a day of very great importance to the country. I hope it will be decided in favor of the Union and liberty. My own dear one went and cast a vote for Lincen. It has been a foggy day.

Nov. 9

Quite unpleasant day but I have been to mill. News the boss had to wait some time. Oh I have heard sad news today. Poor Lucinda Sargent is dead. Alas how sudden.

Nov. 10

Quite a storm in the morning. Frank and I were going to the village but Ella Frick came and interferred with our arrangements. Frank is going to Concord tomorrow. I do hope he will have good success.

Nov. 11

Cold day for poor Frank to go around on his cruches. I carried Frank to the depo. Came home found Mr. Jones and ____ here. Interferred with my plans considerable.

Nov. 12

Not very pleasant day. Frank is pretty tired today. I washed the floors to and expected to bake but Father did not get the flour today. Hes gone off to Cinthes to night.

Nov. 13
Oh what a stormy day. It rained all night and has been snowing all day. Frank cannot go to the village today. He wanted to see Chace Laffers. Mr. Hall went for him. what good did do I guess I would remember if I was Frank.

Nov. 14
It is so afful cold today that I will put off my handwork Oh I am sick tonight. I dont think I shall be able to carry Frank to the depo. Oh dear poor fellow I am so sorry that he has to go to Concord again.

Nov. 15
Oh I am lonesome today and I do feel so worried for fear Frank wont get transferred. It will be too bad to have him go back.

Nov. 16
A cold wintery day. We had a hard snow storm yesterday. Frank and I are going to the village in the sleigh. I have been to the dentist to have my teeth fitted. I do hope I shall get them soon.

Nov. 17
Some warmer to day but it storms tonight. I have been working. Oh my worst fears were verified for my poor lame Frank has to go away. I do think it is two hard and I dont think it is right.

Nov. 18
Baked today. Cold day. Cleaned Frank's coat.

Nov. 19
Quite pleasant. Washed the floors baked and went to the village. Bought 1 1/2 pounds tobacco half pound tea 80 cts... Frank went to. I expect it will be a long time before we ride side together again.

Nov. 20
A verry pleasant day. We have had company all day. Lens folks have been here Jim Farington Betty and Aunt Caroline and I cant remember all. Oh my dear Frank has to go in the morning.

Nov. 21
Oh and a rainy and lonely day this has been. My dearest husban has gone. Oh how lonely I do feel. Poor lame soldier. I hope you will get a long without any trouble.

Nov. 22

A beautiful day. I washed today. Went to mill this afternoon and tonight I find myself with a sore finger and oh so lonesome without my Frank I would like to know wether he was all right tonight.

Nov. 23

Cold day and a stormy night. I am disappointed to night. I expected the dentist and he did not come. I would like to know how Frank fares to night.

Nov. 24

What a splendid Thanksgiving but rather a lonely one to me. If my dear Frank was to home I guess we would have had a good time.

Nov. 25

Beautiful day. Quite a number of callers. Len Spaulding and Fillbrook and my dentist. Oh well I have the much longed for teeth. I don't think I shall like them very well. Mr. Sargent worked here today.

Nov. 26

Another nice day. Went up to the village. Rec twelve dollars and paid Mr. Baily — cts. Bought a quart of oil and a pint of rum. I do hope I shall hear from Frank tonight. I eat dinner at Baileys.

Nov. 27

A rainy day and a lonely one. Oh poor Frank. I know he is lonely. I do wish he could be here tonight. I rec a letter from him tonight and I am going to write back soon.

Nov. 28

Rather cloudy day. Mr. Sargent worked here today. Len this afternoon. Sent Frank a letter. Frankie is not well. Paid 25 cts for medicine 20 c for work to Mr. S and feel very smart tonight.

Nov. 29

A verry warm day for the time of year. been over to Aunt Lee Sargents making her a dress. Did not get it done. I have the blues tonight. I do wish Frank was at home I am so lonely.

Nov. 30

Been a beautiful day. Went to the village this morning. Carried May to school. Cleaned the buttry this afternooon. This is Mays first day at school. Oh I do feel so lonely without my dear Frank.

Dec. 1, 1864

A beautiful day. Been cleaning all the forenoon. Lib Jones came over and is going to stay all night. I rec a letter from my dear Frank. I know he is afful lonesome.

Dec. 2

Quite a pleasant day. Been to work on Aunt Sargents dress. Finished it. Carried it home and went to the village. Called on Mrs. Hopkins. Got May and brought her home. Carried Lib home.

Dec. 3

Is stormy. Snowed last night and rained today. Len been here to day. I have not accomplished much today. Cleaned up my sleeping room. I wish Frank was here to sleep with me tonight.

Dec. 4

Not very pleasant. Hat Sargent here. I do wish they would stay away. Sadie down here. May went home with him to stay all night so as to be there in the morning to go to school.

Dec. 5

Washed today but had an afful sore throat. Dont know but I shall have the dyphera. Hope not. Oh dear I am lonely tonight. I do wish that Frank may come home.

Dec. 6

A prospect of a storm. May has come home. Brought me a letter from dear Pappa. Poor Frank how I pity you. Been up to the village for I don't feel verry smart tonight.

Dec. 7

Went to the village this morning. Carried May to school. Poor little girl. I guess she is lonely tonight. She did not come home it seems and the wind blows and it is a dreary night. Oh I hope it is pleasant where Frank is.

Dec. 8

A cold windy day. The most windy day we have had. I have been to work on my black silk dress. Oh dear I do want Frank to come home so bad.

Dec. 9

The coldest day we have had this season. I went up to the villge this afternoon. Rec a letter from my dear Frank. Poor Frank how I do wish he could be here.

Dec. 10

Woke up this morning and found it snowed and it continues to snow. 10 o'clock at night. I have been so busy on my dress that I have hardly thought of anything else.

Dec. 11

Sunday and a stormy day. Looks quite wintery now. What a lonely day this has been. I do think it is two bad that Frank cant be at home when we want him so much.

Dec. 12

A cold blustry day. Carried my little Mamy to school this morning. I am afraid she is lonely tonight. She is a going to stay at Mrs Baileys this week.

Dec. 13

Cold as Greenland. I have been so busy to work on my dress that I have not stopped for anything. My sholders ach so I dont know what to do. Oh I would like to know if Mr. Tappan said anything to Governor Gillmore.

Dec. 14

Quite pleasant to day. Killed the hog today. Mr. Sargent and Herbut and Unkle came. Went to the village. Got 50 cts sugar. Went to see Mamie. Oh I do wish Frank would come.

Dec. 15

Coldest day of the season. Mr. Sargent been here today desecting the hog. Oh waht a mess it does make to have a hog around. I been to work on my dress.

Dec. 16

Not verry cold day. Washed the floor. Went to the village and brought my little May home. Called to Mr. Pips. Had my dress fitted a little. Rec a letter from dear Frank. Called to Mr. Tappens to know if he had anything for Frank.

Dec. 17

Stormy neather rains nor snow. I dont know what you would call it. Been to work on my dress. Baked six pies and sewed until I am so tired I dont know what to do.

Dec. 18

A splendid day. Lens folks have been here today. I carried them home and also carried May up and left her at Mrs. Bailys. I did not get home until dark.

Dec. 19

Stormy in the morning. Washed put my cothes out. Had to go and get them the wind blew so. Finished my waist and read some to mother. Cold tonight. Oh my poor Frank. I do want you home so bad.

Dec. 20

An afful cold day. Mr. Findheath working here today. Had some trouble with the ᴖld chairs. Rec three letters tonight one from my dear Frank. Oh how lonely he is.

149

Dec. 21

Oh what a storm. I am so provoked. I was going to the village to stay all night. Mrs. Whitcomb and Fritch have been here. I carried them home and incurred the displeasure of Father.

Dec. 22

Oh what a day. The wind blows a hurricane and the snow flies. I was intending to have gone to Concord today but I shall have to wait a while. I do wish Frank was to home this cold night. Oh I do hope it will be warmer tomorrow.

Dec. 23

Oh this a day I've read and have not often seen. I tell you it is cold. Poor little May. How sick she will be. I was to have gone for her tonight but it is ever so cold and we are all blocked up.

Dec. 24

Father has gone to see what can be done to the roads. I hope they will get them broke out for I must go and get Mamie.

Dec. 25

Pleasant day. Been busy day with me. I find my self at the village tonight enroute for Concord. Stayed all night at Mrs Baileys with Mamie.

Dec. 26

I find myself at Concord this dark night and I wish I was at home. I have not accomplished any thing eather. I wish the Gov had been at home. I do want Frank to come home so bad.

Dec. 27

Warm day. Afful sloppy. Came up from Concord today. Stayed all night to Mr. Baileys. Wrote to my dear Frank. I am so tired I don't know.

Dec. 28

Oh what a walk I have had today. Came home from the village. Got my feet just as wet at they could be. It rained quite hard. Made two pairs of drawers since twelve o-clock. I am at home. No place like home.

Dec. 29

Worked on drawers to day. Just as tired as can be but nothing like making money. Warm thawed and verry sloppy.

Dec. 30

Beautiful day. Washed floors and sewed up drawers. Poor May will look for mama tonight but looks in vain for is drawing wood cant have the horse.

Dec. 31

The last day of the year is here. It is verry pleasant but stormed in afternoon. Went to the village. Rec 12 dollars paid out 5 1/2 before I returned home. Carried up 10 pairs of drawers and got 20. Gave Father 4 dollars to pay Herbut. Left me almost ded broke. Thats the way the money goes good bye. I have no more care for this year but I hope to spend many happy days in looking over the past. Hope I shall improve with every year. Good bye.

[On the last page of the diary there are two entries dated earlier in the year:]

Oct. 24

I washed to day and went over to Mrs. Woodbury and have been visiting tonight to Aunts. Oh I would give world if I have them to know that my dear dear Frank was well. oh what a dangerous position he has been in and of it he is spaired how thankful I shall be.

Oct. 25

Went to a meeting up to town hall and oh such a soul stirring speech no one ever heard a better one. It was by the honorable Mr. Potters and oh I do wish I might hear something from Frank.

The remainder of the pages are labeled "account ledger" and are filled with recipes, lists, and accountings, mostly of little interest.

Introduction to Hattie's 1865 Diary

The final diary in the series is Hattie's diary kept during the first half of 1865. It was kept during a time when Frank was in and out of the hospital, often home on leave, although still in the Army. The passages of January of that year are particularly moving as Frank and Hattie both wrote in the diary —sometimes between the lines of each other's entries. There is a clear sense of reunion. They are settling once again into the ordered patterns of domestic life, grateful that his injury will keep him away from the fighting, yet unhappy when they are separated during his frequent returns to the military hospital. Sometimes there are brief glimpses at a resumed sexual relationship. Toward the end of this series, with the coming springtime, there are indications of new life. Hattie's illness in March seems to indicate a possible pregnancy. This is consistent with the oral history in the family that Hattie got pregnant whenever Frank came home on leave. Yet the family birth records do not indicate a birth during this year. More tangible new life occurred, however: Frank planted an orchard that spring and made plans to grow rich on apples. The entries of April 1865 are particularly sombre, as Hattie and Frank reacted to the death of Lincoln and the ending of the war. Once the war was permanently behind them, Hattie, in particular, expressed pent up grief for the horror of the war and the personal loss felt by the mothers, wives—and the soldiers who fought.

Hattie's 1865 diary

Inside flyleaf says: Mrs. Hattie J. Pierce, Bradford, N.H.

Sun., Jan. 1
All hail to a Happy New Year and I hope it is not going to be a specimen of the year. Cold as Greenland and the wind blows hard. I wish my dear Frank was at home this cold New Years night.

Mon., Jan. 2
Very pleasant day. Washed. Made two pairs of drawers. Mr. Field worked here today. I am so disappointed to night. I looked for Frank tonight but he did not come I do wish he would come home.

Tues., Jan. 3 A beautiful day. Sewed on drawers. Carried May up to school. Went to the depot to meet my dear Frank but alas was doomed to disappointment. He did not come.

Weds., Jan. 4
Got up. Found it snowing. It has stoped and it is awful cold to night. I don't see

why I don't hear from Frank. I am so anxious. I don't know what to do.

Thurs., Jan. 5
Ab Graves here today. Cold but pleasant. Cynth came down today. I carried her home. Recd a letter from my dear Frank. I do feel so much better for hearing from him. God help him. Ab is here. Wrote to Frank tonight. Read some.

Fri., Jan. 6
Quite warm. Prospect of a thaw. Frfield worked here to day. I have been making drawers. Work work. I don't see as I am getting very rich very fast.

Sat., Jan. 7
Oh what an awful night. I don't think I ever knew such a night. Mr. Ed Crepsy butchered today. Beef weighed 465 pounds. Mr. Frfield worked here also doing all kinds of work today. Made 2 prs drawers this week.

Sun., Jan. 8
A cold day. Mr. Frfield cut up our beef today. I am glad it is done with. I have been on a continual trot all day. What a man he is. For my part don't like him. Wrote to cousin Sarah tonight.

Mon., Jan. 9
The day of rub a dub here is gone but I failed to wash to day owing to events such as wash tumbs being in use. Been busy though. Ab went away this morning.

Tues., Jan. 10
An awful stormy day. Rained and hailed. I looked for my dear Frank but am doomed to disappointment. Oh I do wish he would come home. Mr. Frfield has been here salting our beef.

Weds., Jan. 11
Cold day. Went to the village. Took back the drawers and brought them home. Was sewing very busy when who should I see but my dear husband. How glad I am.

Thurs., Jan. 12
I am so glad my dear Husband has returned. Been sewing on drawers. Be glad when I get them done. Want to visit with my dear Frank.
Do you indeed love me so much my dear Hat? [written in Frank's hand]

Fri., Jan. 13
A cold day. Washed today. Rather late in the week but better late than never. Frank God bless him is at home. How glad I am. I do love to have him at home.
[Frank's hand] And I love to be with you dear wife, Frank

Sat., Jan. 14
Storms today. Frank and I was going to the village. Stormed so we could'nt go Mr. Frfield came to work but went home again. Finished drawers today. Frank says I shant do any more.
[Frank's hand] Yes and I mean it.

Sun., Jan. 15
Cold and windy. Snow flying awfully. Will be drifted badly I expect. Uncle Commings is here. Also Hurbert and late in the day Len made his appearance. To night we poped corn.

Mon., Jan. 16
Cold and windy. Frank and I have to postpone our going to the village. Don't care for my part. I dont see what makes me so cross to day I am sure. I hope I shall feel better in the morning.

Tues., Jan. 17
17th day of January. My birthday. I hope I shall grow to be a better woman before a nother birthday. Frank and I went to the village to day. Called to see Hadley. An awful cold day.
[Frank's hand] You are a good woman now Hat far better than I am but I love you [drawing of a heart] so dearly Hat— Frank.

Weds., Jan. 18
[Frank's hand] A cold dreary day. At home all day. Had enough to do to keep warm. Hat says I must do the writing in her Diary while at home. I think she is big enough to do her own writing. But here goes. Hat pretty good natured all day.

Thurs., Jan. 19
[Frank's hand] We got up this morning about nign o.c. and found another cold day. At home all day and Hat somewhat X and a little unwell. She had better look out—she is making a dress for Frankie and I well doing nothing all day.

Fri., Jan. 20
[Frank's hand] A very cold day. Started to go to the village but got stuck in a snow drift and had to turn back. Hat somewhat disappointed. She has been sewing on the children's dresses and as for me I have been doing nothing all day hard.

Sat., Jan. 21
[Frank's hand] A pleasant day but rather cool. Hat and I went up to the village after noon and went to Len's for a visit at night. Len gone over after a load of wood. Got home about 5 p.m. and after supper he and I went to the village.

Sun., Jan. 22

[Frank's hand] Got up about 9 AM and found Len and Cynth in a stew for fear Gould would come before we eat breakfast. O don't Hat and me like to sleep in the morning! Len poped some corn. Hat eat about a peck as usual. I didn't eat any. O no not any. Started for home abut 5 pm. Some signs of snow.

Mon., Jan. 23

[Frank's hand] Got up about 9 as usual and found it snowing. Had quite a time getting redy to go to E. W. but it stormed so hard had to give it up. Hat got a little mad and so did I and we didn't spend a very pleasant day together. I think it to bad don't you Hat? Made up at night as usual.

Tues., Jan. 24

[Frank's hand] Got up this morning at 9 and here I must say one word about our time last night. Didn't we enjoy ourselves Hat? 8 o.c. and all is well. Sam Hall here to night. Hat working on mother's dress. All I have done to day is to put some rockers on the cradle for children.

Weds., Jan. 25

[Frank's hand] Got up this morning at 9 as usual and found a pleasant day but quite cold. Went and shoveled out Hat's clothes line and helped her put out her clothes. Father has been up to Mr. Halls and says they are not going to open the road today.

[Hattie's hand resumes here] Thurs., Jan. 26

A pretty cold day. Started for E. Washington about 3 p.m. Arrived there about 5. Found all well. Had a good time. Staid at Tom Peasleys. I never was so cold as when I arrived at E W. Coldest night we have had this year.

Fri., Jan. 27

Another cold day. Got up this morning at 8. Oh how afful cold. went up to Carys after dinner. Staid untill after ten and went to see a much cherished friend from my old native town.

Sat., Jan. 28

Cold as ever this morning. Staid to Toms last night. Had a very pleasant evening with our old friend Ellry Davis. Came right from my dear old home. I can't tell how glad I am to see him. It was an unexpected suprise meeting him here.

Sun., Jan. 29

I don't think it is quite so cold this morning. We start for B today. Had a grand good visit. I guess our folks think we have run away. Arived at home all right. Found Len's folks here a little out of sorts at our absence.

Mon., Jan. 30

Cold as Greenland Got up about as usual. Expected to wash but had to give it up. Went to the village in the forenoon and up to Unkle Commins in the afternoon. Had a good visit. Got some cider that made it so interesting.

Tues., Jan. 31

Not quite so cold. Washed today. Father gone to a pedling at Sanders today. Frank is busy doing chores. Rather an uphappy day. Frank don't love me to day. I always feel unhappy when my dear Frank is distant. So tired tonight.

Weds., Feb. 1

Not quite so pleasant as yesterday. Frank gave up going tomorrow. I am glad he will be with us an other day. Father arrived safe today. Sold all his handles at the bridge. Staid at E.W. Sold better he expected. Been a happy day. Frank loves me to day.

Thurs., Feb. 2

An afful windy day. We are going to the village to stay all night. Frank going in the morning. How lonely we will be. Had a afful time getting through the drifts. Thought we would have to give it up.

Fri., Feb. 3

Cold morning. Had to get up early this morning. Frank left us this morning. How lonely it seems. Went to the depo and then to the dentists. Fixed my teeth. Made some calls. Came back to Cynths. I felt so lonely and blue. I was glad to get home. Got through better than I expected.

Sat., Feb. 4

A very pleasant day I do feel so lonesome without Frank. Been verry busy ever since I got up wich by the way was in the forenoon. Ironed and mended all day. Been reading to night. So ends the week.

Sun., Feb. 5

Stormy day. Wrote a letter to Brother. Read the rest of the time. Len and Sam Hall was in. I have been verry lonesome today with my dear Husban gone.

Mon., Feb. 6

Pleasant day. Washed this forenoon. Went to Cinthas in the afternoon. Went to the village before I went to Cinthas. going to stay a day or two. Rec'd a letter from Frank.

Tues., Feb. 7

Been sewing all day. Went to the depo to meet Frank but was disappointed. He did not come. I am sorry Len oten [probably means "ought not to have"] went off home and left us at the depo.

Weds., Feb. 8

Oh what a snowstorm. The most that has fallen at any one time this winter. Len has been shoveling snow all morning. Cynth is not verry well. I find it verry lonely. I shall be glad when tomorrow comes. I am going home.

Thurs., Feb. 9

A verry pleasant day but cold. Rode up to the store with Doctor Fisk in the morning. He came into see Cynth. Came home to night and am glad to get home I expect. I expect my dear Frank home tomorrow night.

Fri., Feb. 10

Cold raw day. Have not accomplshed much today. Read most all day in Rutlige. My Dear has come. I am so glad he has come. Mrs. Spaulding has come with him. I was not expecting her but am glad to see her.

Sat., Feb. ll

Cold and windy. Finished mending my dress. We talked of going to the village. Thought it to cold. Gave it up. Baked in the afternoon. Sam Hall came in looking rather hard. Frank been to work on ax handles to day.

Sun., Feb. 12

A nother cold day. Frank, Mrs. Spaulding and my self went for a ride. Stoped at Lens a little while. Came home eat dinner and found the day most gone. Mrs. S. starts in the morning.

Mon., Feb. 13

Cold cold. Did ever any one see such a cold time? The coldest night we have had this year. Frank and I carried Mrs. S. to the depo. We almost froze. We were glad to get home. Found it drifted some. don't think Frank can get away in the morning.

Tues., Feb. 14

A very cold day. I feel lonely to night. Frank is going in the morning. I shall feel verry lonely when he is gone. I do wish he could stay home. Mother is packing his velice. I had to [illegible]

Weds., Feb. 15

The nicest day we have had for a long time. Frank went off this morning. I do feel so lonesome to night. Ella Fitch and Walter been here to day. Mr. Frfield took dinner with us.

Thurs., Feb. 16

Snow snow. It snowed last night. Could not possably get along without snow. If it follows in the line of the programe it will blow a hurricane to morrow. I hope not. I am going to the village if it is pleasant. The old insurance man came to day.

Fri., Feb. 17

Cold day. Cleaned up the front room. Am all ready to go to the village. Father is getting the horse. Went to the village. Rec a letter from my Dear Husban and also from cousin Sarrah. Ella went with me.

Sat., Feb. 18

Cold and windy. Havn't accomplished much to day. Been sewing all day. Sam Hall came in the evening. Brought me a letter from Concord. Oh how long it seems since Dear Frank went a way.

Sun., Feb. 19

Pretty cold day but not to cold for Hat Sargent to come. I do wish that tribe would stay away. Been a lonesome day. I am so lonesome Sundays when my Deer Frank is gone. Written four letters to day and read some.

Mon., Feb. 20

Cold and windy. Washed a two weeks washing and pretty tired to night. Been reading out loud and I am afraid its to late to do much writing to night after 9 o clock.

Tues., Feb. 21

A beautiful day. Went to the village. Came home about dark. Who should come but Ed, Carrie Peasley and Nate Jones? Had to stay all night the road was so bad.

Weds., Feb. 22

A nother pleasant day. Company went away early this morning. Ironed and sewed on my militon. Sam been down here to night.

Thurs., Feb. 23

Pleasant day. Have felt very unwell to day and yesterday. Went to the village. Bought a barrel of flower and carried up my waist to have some buttonholes worked.

Fri., Feb. 24

Nice day. Don't feel very well to day. Washed the floors to day. Was just foolish enough to look for my Dear husban but I am afraid I shall have to look for some time before I see him.

Sat., Feb. 25
A very pleasant day. Went to the village to get my money. Waited for my Deer Frank but he did not come. I was so disappointed. I do wish that he would come. Rec 12 dollars and paid out our two.

Sun., Feb. 26
Waked up this morning and found it stormy. Glad it was rain instead of snow. Had a nough snow. Hope we shant have any more. Sent a letter to Frank by Len. Cousin Anna and Ella Fitch came in for a few minutes.

Mon., Feb. 27
An afful windy day. I thought it to bad a day to work. I have been to work on my militone. Got it about done. I been reading some to night and cut Frankie a dress out.

Tues., Feb. 28
An afful cold and gloomy day. Cut out Mamies apren and went to the village this afternoon. Waited for the mail. Had an afful snowstorm to come home in but rec a good long letter from my Dear Frank that paid me.

Weds., Mar. 1
Quite pleasant. Washed. Len folks were here to dinner. Chet Spaulding came and mother and I had quite a cry. Wrote to Frank.

Thurs., Mar. 2
Cold and windy. Mr. King came here to have Father sign a petition for the mail agincy. Father signed it.

Fri., Mar. 3
How do you do my Deer and good old Friend? It has been such a long time since I have had any conversation with that I afraid you will think I have been rather neglectful but I am going to tell you what I have been doing all this long time. [Sat. 4] It has got to be the 11 of the month. Frank came home the 3 of the month and poor fellow he was sick. [Sun. 5] He had to go right to bed. He walk from Melvins Hill and that was to much for him. I think Mr. Wheeler showed himself a hog never offered to bring him home and Frank was so tired he didn't [Mon. 6] know what to do. He wasnt much better the next day. Sunday took some medicine. Len folks came down. Father carried them home and got some whisky, 70 cts pint. Frank better in the morning. Washed some.

Tues., Mar. 7
I washed Tuesday 7. Mother and Aunt Cather went to Unkle Comens. Frank and I kept house. I made my new skirt. They gave Mothers Aunt Polly nice black dress.

I baked pottatoes and broiled steak. Frank [Weds. 8] eat so much I think they hurt him. He was taken worse again. We went to the villige. I wanted him to see the doctor but he would not.

Thurs., Mar. 9
Lucette bought Aunt a dress. The neighbors subscribed and so bought her the dress. I cut it the 9 and and finished it the 10. Frank worked on ax handles.

Fri., Mar. 10
Frank not verry well. The weather stormy. We went to the village.

Sat., Mar. 11
Qite pleasant. Father went off pedling ax handles. I washed the floors baked and went to Mr. Halls on an errand. Felt verry unwell at night.

Sun., Mar. 12
What an affuld. I was taken with a verry bad Diarhea and was sick all day. Never had it before. Guess I caught it from Frank. Father came home to day. Almost froze. I am sick.

Mon., Mar. 13
Cold day. Frank went for the doctor. Was afraid I was going to have inflammation. The doctor came. Said I was pretty sick. Don't think he knows verry much.

Tues., Mar. 14
Qite pleasant. This is the day for the state election. Frank rode up with the doctor. He says I am better. Of course he must know. I know I don't think the shits is verry funny.

Weds., Mar. 15
Wednesday. Feel some better. Mrs. Fitch came in to see me. She is the only person that has been in. Frank has got to go in the morning. How lonely I shall be.

Thurs., Mar. 16
Frank went this morning and oh how lonely I am. Been affal sick to day. Not so smart as I was yesterday and I did feel so to have Frank go away.

Fri., Mar. 17
No better to day. Len came down brought me some lemons that my Deer Frank sent me. They tasted good the best of any thing that I have tried to eat.

Sat., Mar. 18
I feel much better to day. Guess I am going to be smart again. Don't feel verry

hungry yet. Hope my appetite will come soon.

Sun., Mar. 19
Keep gaining some but dont feel verry smart yet. Do wish I could eat. Been verry much interested in reading a story in the weekly.

Mon., Mar. 20
Monday. Washing day. Don't feel well enoguth to wash. Len moving to day. He brought me some bitters. Hope it will help me. I am to work on an old dress

Tues., Mar. 21
A splendid day. Len finished moving to day. Ana Pierce spent the afternoon here. I havent got my dress done. Cynth came in with her Lambs. I am feeling better.

Weds., Mar. 22
Rained all day. Finished my dress. Went up to Cynths to see how she looked in her new house. Hurbut brought me a letter from Frank. I was glad to hear from my Dearest Husban. I wish it had been his own Dear self.

Thurs., Mar. 23
Didn't accomplish much to day. Worked on mothers dress. Had a terrible sick headache. Couldn't eat any of mothers baken beans. Couldnt eat my supper.

Fri., Mar. 24
Been a verry busy day with me. Washed the floor and baked. My Dear Frank came home to night. He brought me lots of goodies but I think more of seeing his dear self. He is looking well.

Sat., Mar. 25
Did not rise verry early. Had such a good bed fellow. Went to the villige. Paid our bills $30 to Carr. 10.59 to Moss [illegible] to corner. Came home found Hank Sargent here. Said Lib Jones married.

Sun., Mar. 26
Cold raw day. We went to Hurbuts. Staid most all day. Had a verry good visit. We called to our Dear little Evas grave the first time this spring. Dearest little angel how we miss she.

Mon., Mar. 27
Verry nice day. Went to Mr. Felthes on a tom fool errand. Heard he had a little Lamb to give away but found he hadn't. Spoiled the day. Len worked for Frank in the forenoon and Frank helped him in the afternoon.

Tues., Mar. 28
A beautiful day. Frank went back this morning. It seems verry lonesome but I have been so busy I didn't have much time to be lonely. I washed to day.

Weds., Mar. 29
A verry nice day. Went to Mrs Tichs a visiting. Took both the childrens. Wrote to sister Pine last night. Was in hopes to have sent it to day but did not.

Thurs., Mar. 30
Len waked me up this morning crying. I heard it raining. Had a good mind not to get up. Cleared off. I went to the village in the afternoon. Rec a letter from Dear Frank. Found the auction all gone.

Fri., Mar. 31
This has been a stormy day. Rained all day. I have been busy all day. Wrote to Frank this morning. Ironed out Frankie a dress and May an apron. Went to Cynthas. Rec a letter from Frank. Read all the eve.

Sat., April 1
Been qite pleasant day. Qite diffrent from last year at this time. I have busy all day. Aunt Amy Sam Hall and Ella Fitch have been here today. I finished Frankies dress and Mays apron.

Sun., April 2
Cold and windy. Been at home all day. Oh no went to Mrs. Halls to get Cyntha some milk for her lambs. Setty came down for some papers. Wrote a letter to Frank. Sent it to Frank Cressy. Frankies not very well.

Mon., April 3
A nice day. I have been to Sutten to Chesters and I am so tired I don't know what to do. I hope Aunt will be well treated. I feel as though I could not sympathise with any one to night.

Tues., April 4
Rather cold day. Washed cleaned up the shed. Mos afful tired. Went to fussing with my lamp and broke it and what was worse spilt the oil on the floor and myself two. So tired when I got the mess clean up.

Weds., April 5
Rained a little this morning. Just enough to keep me from washing the floor. Ironed and baked. Looked for my Dear soldier but he did not come. I do hope he will come to morrow night.

Thurs., April 6
[Frank's hand] Arrived at home today on a 30 days furlough. Found Hat at the village with the horse so I got a ride home. Hat says she is glad to see me. Don't know aobut that. I was glad to see her anyway. Frank

Fri., April 7
[Frank's hand] A very pleasant day. Mr. Frfield worked for father in the forenoon drawing wood. For my part I haven't done much of anything hard all day. I think Hat will get sick of having me write for her.

Sat., April 8
[Frank's hand] Pretty cold day Len worked for us today drawing wood. y.c. I don't know what Hat has been doing today She is not very well. Plowd the Garden today. I got a little coss tonight and Hat says I swear awfully. Don't know but I shall have to go down to the Pond and get converted.

Sun., April 9
[Frank's hand] Cool with some signs of rain. Hat and I went out for a little ride. Went over to Mr. Cressys to see Warren who got work on the RR.

Mon., April 10
[Frank's hand] A cold stormy day. Didn't do much today. Len and I started to go over to Warner after trees but give it up. Hat was glad of it I suppose. She was some mad because we went I guess weren't you Hat? Frank.

Tues., April 11
[Frank's hand] Pleasant but cool. Len worked for us cutting wood besid the Road. I guess Hat is in better humor today. Good news from the Army. Richmond has fallen. Frank.

Weds., April 12
[Frank's hand] Rather wet and rainy. Helped make a gate Y.c. Nothing new today. Frank.

Thurs., April 13
[Frank's hand] A pleasant day. Hurbert and Len helped us plow in the afternoon. Len helped cut wood in the forenoon. Frank.

Friday, April 14
[Frank's hand] A pleasant day. Done some grafting in the forenoon. Hat and I went up to the village afternoon. Paid Frfield $3.25

Sat., April 15
[Hattie's hand] A pleasant day but rather cold. Len worked here in the forenoon. Frank worked for Len in the afternoon. Oh what sad news we have heard our Dier President is dead and shot oh dier can't be.

Sun., April 16.
[Hattie's hand] Cold day. Quite a number in to day but all seem sad. What a sad sabbath all over the Country. Frank and I went to Mr Hacks. There is no more room for doubt as much beloved President is gone.

Mon., April 17
[Hattie's hand] Pleasant day. Washed and cleaned some. Hurbut here to work to day half past 10. Frank and Len are fishing. I do wish they would come home for I am sleepy. I don't think I will sit up long. Cynth been here to night.

Tues., April 18
[Frank's hand] Quite cool winds and some signs of rain. Worked hard all day whitewashing. Hat cleaning house. Len worked for Uncle Cummings. Len and I got a good mess of fish last night. Frank.

Weds., April 19
[Hattie's hand resumes] A day of mourning all over the county. We attended the furnel service of our much beloved President to. Oh what a sad time. Mr. Toffen speak well. Was much interested.

Thurs., April 20 and Fri. 21
Finished cleaning to day. Worked afful hard this week. We can't think of nothing but the great loss our beloved country has met with. The merdr [sic] has escaped but will be caught in all probabilty. I cincerly hope so. I dont remember just what we have been doing today so I wont make any attempt.

Sat., April 22
A very warm day. Frank and I went to the village. Bought May an Frankie some shoes. Quite late when we got home. Frank and Len went fishing. Caught 39 fish.

Sun., April 23
Cold as greneland to day. Thought of going to the Baptizing but dont feel well enough. Father and May went and they almost froze. Havent hardly stired to day.

Mon., April 24 [April 24 - April 29 run together]
Washed as usul. Aways rub a dub dub on Monday that everlasting wash day will always presit in coming better be Monday. [Tues. 24] I for my part sincerly thank first the lady that invented Monday for Wash day. I beg pardon dear Dieria for

164

neglecting you so but I know if you new all I had to do you would freely pardon me. [Weds. 26] This has been the most forward spring I have known since I have been in New England and the most pleasant one. Frank has been home on 30 days furlough and we hear that [Thurs. 27] the war is almost over. What a good sound that word has to the many poor soldiers wives and lonely mothers and oh wont the poor soldiers Rejoice no more Bloody Battles.

Fri., April 28
What sadness comes with all our joys. If our Dear President could have lived to see all his good works fullfilled but God is just and doeth all things for the best. [Sat. 29] How many lonely wives and mothers there are tonight thinking if he could only lived untill now but they have given their lives for a holy cause. Peace be to their ashes.

Sun., April 30
Cold day. Frank and I went to Unkle Chapans. Staid for dinner. Called to Aunt Susans.

Mon., May 1
Washed. Went to see Mr. Hall. Anna called in. Frank and Len washed their great orchard. Expect they will make their fortune raising apples. Rained. Had qite a shower.

Tues., May 2
Frank's birthday. Meant to have gone to the village and bought Frank a present but it rained so I could not go. I was at Concord a year ago to day and now my old soldier is at home with me.

Weds., May 3
Unkle Comens plowed here this forenoon. Looked for Aunt Caroline but she did not come. Cyntha took supper with us. Len to work for Frank up to Unkles.

Thurs., May 4
A verry pleasant day. Mothers birthday. Wish I could get her something. Aunt came this afternoon and also Mrs. Spaulding and my Dear old Friend Mrs. Chamberlain. How sad she seemed.

Fri., May 5
Mrs. Spaulding went away this morning. Mrs. C and I carried her to the depo. Frank has been doing little jobs round the house all day. He moved the old clock.

Sat., May 6
Qite lonesome to day. Mrs. C. has gone off with Dear Frank and I miss my Dear

165

old soldier boy. He has been home so long that the house seems afful lonely.

Sun., May 7
This has been an afful lonely day and qite cold. I slept away a goodeal of the day. Dug some Dandelions. Called in to Mrs. Hall. I wonder if Dear Frank misses me as much as I do him.

Mon., May 8
Done an afful great wash. Mr. Sargent came in about dinner time. I went to the village. Rec a letter from Dear Frank. Shall expect him home soon.

Tues., May 9
Rained all day but the sun has set clean. I guess it will be pleasant tomorrow. I wish I knew whether there was a letter for me or not. Have not done much to day. Had Greens for dinner.

Weds., May 10
Quite pleasant this morning but cold as Greneland to night. Been to Sutten to day and also to the villige and I am as tired as the dog to night. Spent 2.15 cts to day.

Thurs., May 11
Woke up found it raining. Ironed to day. Went down to Mrs. Chenys on a Tom fool errand. Cut out Addies coat. Rec a letter from Frank to night.

Fri., May 12
Rained all the forenoon. Mrs. Fitch Family here. I wanted to go to Manchester but it rained to hard. I dont know what to do. Hope Frank will be home tomorrow night.

Sat., May 13
Almost ten o clock. Been a beautiful day. Wish I had gone to Manchester. Was in hope that Frank would come home to night but was doomed to disappointment. Worked hard to day.

Sun., May 14
A splendid day. Havent done much to day but putter around. Hasnt been any one here to day. Think of going to Concord to morrow if I dont change my mind.

Mon., May 15
A Beautiful day. Len worked for Father this afternooon. I washed. I meant to have gone to Manchester but give it up. Dont see why Frank dont come home.

Tues., May 16
Splendid day. Been cleaning house. Oh how tired I am to night. Len planted corn

to day. Father helped him. I am glad the front room is cleaned up.

Weds., May 17
The warmest day we have had. I dropped oer to day the first I ever dropped. Picked greens and ironed and I am so tired I dont know what to do so I'll go to bed.

Thurs., May 18
Cold and windy. Finished my hoop skirt. Went to the village expect to start to Manchester. I am afful cold. Wish my Dear Frank was here to sleep with me.

Fri., May 19
Cold and rainy. Got all ready to start for M. Rained so I gave it up. Been patching all day. Oh I forgot I had a fine cry. I never did see such a gloomy time.

Sat., May 20
There was a prospect this morning of fair weather and I started for Manchester but we cant always tell and I had a rainy day. Didn't find Frank at the depo. Was home sick enough. Went to the hospital [Sun. 21] found Frank. We went to Mrs. Toan's. Had a verry pleasant visit. Didn't relish going to Aunt Sturcts much but went. Rained all night. Went to the Cemetry.

Mon., May 22
Oh I was disappointed this morning. Found it raining. Went out done some shopping. Frank went to the Hospital. I went to Mrs. Towns. Had a good time. Started for Concord 5 p.m.

Tues., May 23
Rained as usual. Rains all the time. Didn't enjoy me self verry well. Glad I am going home. Mrs. Chamberlain went to the depo with me. I am home once more and I feel thankful. Father met me at the Depo.

Weds., May 24
Glad to find myself at home. It does tire me to go visiting affuly. I have been sick today. It has been a beautiful day. Been digging greens.

Thurs., May 25
A splendid morning. Had company all day. Maggie Sargent and Abbe Drugan finished picking my greens. Had boil dish for dinner. Feel tired tonight.

Fri., May 26
Rather pleasant day. Went the villige. Got my hat trimed. Father went with me. Called and got my twelve dollars. Walked home. Was in hopes to have heard something from Frank.

Sat., May 27
Cold day. Been sewing all day. Cyntha been boiling soap this afternoon. I do wish Frank would come home. I should think he would write.

Sun., May 28
A rainy day. Not done much to day. Made a corn starch pudding for dinner the first I ever made. Hat Sargent came in. I trimed her Hat. I do wish my Dear Frank was here to night.

Mon., May 29
A rainy day. Washed. Went to the villige. I thought I should get a letter but no letter nor no Husban but I heard from him through Frank Cressy.

Tues., May 30
A splendid day. Mr. Cheny worked here to day this fornoon. Paid him two dollars for half days work. Been making my Dress shorter. I don't see why Frank dont come home.

Weds., May 31
Quite pleasant. Havent accomplished much to day. Went to the villige at night. Rec a letter from Frank. Was in hopes he would come. Dont see why he cant.

Thurs., June 1
A splendid day and a day of mourning for our good President. I should liked to have gone to Concord but it always happens so I cant go any where when I want to.

Fri., June 2
A splendid day. Went up had the children photo taken and had a pretty hot time. Walked most all the way and part the way back.

Sat., June 3
A nice day. Feel pretty well used up. Mamie is sick. Over done yesterday. Frank came home to night with his Discharge in his pocket. Glad to have his freedom once more.

Sun., June 4
The warmest day we have had this season. Have not been out to day. No one been here to stop oh yes Anna P has been here. Warm to night.

Mon., June 5
A nice day. Washed and swept the Chamber and went to the villige. Franks clothes

came. I was afraid they were lost.

Tues., June 6
A verry warm day. Washed wollen to day. Our ould Hog is sick she is so Frank going to sit up with her. I am afraid she wont do well.

Weds., June 7
An other warm day. The old Hog is sick yet. Mr. Feltck worked here to day. Mrs. Cressy helped to fix our Lounge to day. it is a gooddeal work.

Thurs., June 8
An afful warm day. Went over to Mrs. Cressys to measure my cushion. Am afful [illegible].

[next page:] recipes for French polish and "wash for the head."
Accounts and lists are on adjoining pages.

[In the Memoranda section, there is a two-page entry, undated:]

Have taken 30 pairs drawers carried back 10 pairs returned 20 pairs of drawers again 10 pairs more but dont think I shall make them for they found fault with the lot. I dont like to be found fault with my self especly for such small wages. Oh would Frank Laugh and say it was good enough for me though I was making money so fast. That is the was with the Wesley way. All our bright prospects is crushed in the bud.

[Entries from both Hattie and Frank appear on the next page.]

[Hattie's hand] Frank and I have been having a little Discussion about our favorite writers. I maintain that Mrs. Southworth is far the best but Frank says nay that Cob's much better but I dont find the point and I dont see any use in prolonging this discussion so we will adjourn to night to resume at some future hearing.

[Frank's hand] I think but little of either of them but of the two I prefer Cobb, for a cob may be useful to strike by with and Mrs. S. can be much no possible use of.

Lists and a cookie recipie appear on the next pages. In the pocket at the back of the book is a letter to Frankie. It is addressed to "Miss B. Frank Pierce" on the outside. The letter, itself, reads as follows:

Darling little daughter
Mama says I must write a letter to you, and so I will do so and put it in her letter and now what shall I say to you. Has little Frankie been a good girl since Papa left home? I hope she has for I shall bring her a new dollie when I come and I should feel badly if I had to give it to a naughty girl. But I guess she is a good girl, and she must

169

kiss mama for papa and when she says her prayers at night at Mama knee, she must remember to pray for papa and must write a letter to me. Good night little darling. Papa would give any thing if he could see you tonight.

Papa

ENDNOTES

Chapter One

1. Augustus Ayling, *Revised Register of the Soldiers and Sailors of New Hampshire in the War of Rebellion* (Concord: Ira C. Evans, Printer, 1895), p. 693.

2. David Hackett Fischer, *Albion's Seed* (New York: Oxford University Press, 1989), p. 204.

3. Article from family records.

4. Benjamin Franklin Pierce, Military Records, U. S. Archives.

5. Francis Buffum, *A Memorial of the Great Rebellion: Being A History of The Fourteenth Regiment New Hampshire Volunteers* (Boston: Franklin Press, 1882), p. 397.

6. Buffum p. 397.

7. Burke Davis, *The Civil War: Strange and Fascinating Facts* (New York: Fairfax Press, 1982), p. 63.

8. Buffum p. 20.

9. Francis Dyer, *Compendium of the War of the Rebellion* (Dayton, Ohio: Press of Morningside Bookshop, 1908), p. 1352.

Chapter Two

1. Buffum p. 693.

2. Community Telephone and Business Directory (Poolesville: Poolesville Area Chamber of Commerce, 1991), pp. 67-69.

3. James Robertson, *Tenting Tonight* (Alexandria, Va.: Time-Life Books, Inc., 1984), p. 62.

4. Fischer p. 251.

5. Davis p. 59.

6. Buffum pp. 398, 416.

7. Buffum pp. 398, 416.

8. Buffum pp. 398, 416.

9. Buffum p. 442.

10. Pierce, Military Records, U. S. Archives.

11. Fischer pp. 150-151.

12. Margaret Leech, *Reveille In Washington, 1860-65* (New York: Harper and Row, 1941), pp. 141-150. Francis Miller, *The Photographic History of the Civil War* (New York: Thomas Yoseloff, Inc., 1957), p. 289.

Chapter Three

1. *The War of Rebellion: Official Records of the Union and Confederate Armies* (Washington: Government Printing Office, 1893), Vol. XXXIII, p. 473.

2. Buffum p. 411.

3. Official Records, Vol. XXIII, p. 487.

4. Ayling p. 694.

5. Ayling pp. 694-695.

6. Ayling pp. 694-695.

7. Ayling pp. 694-695.

Chapter Four

1. Mildred Gunscheon, Sr. Editor, *Two Hundred Plus: Bradford, New Hampshire in Retrospect* (Canaan, New Hampshire: Phoenix Publishing, 1976), p. 93ff.

2. D. Hamilton Hurd, Ed., *History of Merrimack and Belknap Counties, New Hampshire* (Philadelphia: J. W. Lewis & Co., 1885), p. 207.

3. Hurd p. 205.

4. Gunscheon p. 20.

5.   Fischer p. 136.

6.   Gunscheon p. 116.

Chapter Five

1.   Gene Smith, *Lee and Grant* (Secaucus, N. J.: The Blue and Gray Press, 1984), p. 219.

2.   James McPherson, *The Battle Cry of Freedom* (New York: Oxford University Press, 1988), p. 757.

3.   Joseph Whitehorne, *The Battle of Cedar Creek* (Strasburg, Va.: The Wayside Museum of American History and Arts, 1987), p. 15.

4.   Brandon Beck and Charles Grunder, *Three Battles of Winchester* (Berryville, Va.: The Country Publishers, 1988), p. 3.

5.   Whitehorne p. 5.

6.   *Official Records*, Vol. XLIII, pp. 318-319.

7.   Ayling p. 694.

8.   *Official Records*, Vol. XLIII, pp. 325-326.

9.   Shelby Foote, *The Civil War: A Narrative*. Vol. III, "Red River to Appomattox" (New York: Random House, 1974), p. 555, n. 3.

10. Buffum pp. 420-425.

11. Foote p. 563.

12. From a conversation of Daniel Biles with a parishioner recalling a story handed down from his ancestors.

13. Whitehorn p. 13.

14. *Official Records*, Vol. XLIII, pp. 322-323.

15. Ayling p. 694.

16. Norton Boothe, *Great Generals of the Civil War And Their Battles* (New York: Bison Books Corp., 1986), p. 178.

Chapter Six

1. Gunscheon p. 248.

2. Gunscheon pp. 72-73.

3. Ayling p. 694.

4. Ayling p. 694.

5. Ayling p. 695.

Epilogue

1. Pierce, Military Records, U.S. Archives.

2. Pierce, Military Records, U.S. Archives.

3. Newspaper Clipping among family articles, unidentified source.

BIBLIOGRAPHY

Benjamin F. and Harriett G. Pierce

Family Records: Letters, Newspaper Clippings, Oral History, etc.

Pierce, Benjamin F. 1863 Dairy.

Pierce, Benjamin F. Military Records. U. S. Archives.

Pierce, Harriett G. 1864 Diary, 1865 Diary.

Bradford, New Hampshire

Fischer, David Hackett. *Albion's Seed*. New York: Oxford University Press, 1989.

Gunscheon, Margaret, Sr., ed. *Two Hundred Plus: Bradford, New Hampshire in Retrospect*. Canaan, N. H.: Phoenix Publishing, 1976.

Civil War

Ayling, Augustus. *Revised Register of the Soldiers and Sailors of New Hampshire in the War of Rebellion*. Concord, N.H.: Ira C. Evans, Printer, 1895.

Biles, Daniel. *A Soldier's Journey*. Gettysburg, Pa.: Thomas Publications, 1990.

Beck, Brandon and Charles Grunder. *Three Battles of Winchester*. Berryville, Va.: The Country Publishers, 1988.

Billings, John. *Hard-Tack and Coffee*. Boston: George Smith and Co., 1887.

Boothe, F. Norton. *Great Generals of the Civil War and Their Battles*. New York: Bison Books Corp., 1986.

Buffum, Francis. *A Memorial of the Great Rebellion: Being a History of the Fourteenth New Hampshire Volunteers*. Boston: Franklin Press, 1882.

Davis, Burke. *The Civil War: Strange and Fascinating Facts*. New York: Fairfax Press, 1982.

Dyer, Francis. *Compendium of the War of Rebellion*. Dayton, Oh.: Press of the Morningside Bookshop, 1908.

Foote, Shelby. *The Civil War: A Narrative*. Volume III: "Red River to Appomattox." New York: Random House, 1974.

Frew, James. *Civil War Battles in Winchester and Frederick County, Virginia, 1861-1865*. Winchester-Frederick County Historical Society, 1961.

Leech, Margaret. *Reveille in Washington, 1860-65*. New York: Harper and Row, 1941.

McPherson, James. *Battle Cry of Freedom*. New York: Oxford University Press, 1988.

Miller, Francis. T*he Photographic History of the Civil War*. New York: Thomas Yoseloff, Inc., 1957.

Robertson, James. *Tenting Tonight*. Alexandria, Va.: Time-Life Books, Inc., 1984.

Smith, Gene. *Lee and Grant*. Secaucus, N. J.: The Blue and Gray Press, 1984.

Stern, Philip. *Soldier Life in the Union and Confederate Armies*. Bloomington, Ind.: Indiana University Press, 1961.

_____. *The War of Rebellion: Official Records of the Union and Confederate Armies*. Washington: Government Printing Office, 1893.

Ward, Geoffrey. *The Civl War*. New York: Alfred A. Knopf, Inc., 1990.

Welcher, Frank. *The Union Army, 1861-1865*. Volume I: The Eastern Theatre. Indianapolis: The Indiana University Press, 1989.

Whitehorne, Joseph. *The Battle of Cedar Creek*. Strasburg, Va.: The Wayside Museum of American History and Arts, 1987.

ABOUT THE AUTHORS

Sheila Murnane Cumberworth, great-great granddaughter of Franklin and Harriett Pierce, was born in Minneapolis, Minnesota, in 1947. She was raised in the home that her great-grandparents had built in the late 1800s on Bald Eagle Lake, just outside of White Bear Lake, Minnesota. Her immediate neighbors and closest companions were cousins and other family members. When she was 16 years old, her family left Minnesota and moved to Orchard Park, New York, where she finished high school in 1965.

Returning to Minnesota, Sheila attended Carleton College and graduated in 1969. She married a Carleton classmate, Mitch Cumberworth, that same year and moved with him to Ann Arbor, Michigan. She has two daughters, Bethany Jane (born in 1971), and Anne Kinsley (born in 1974). In 1983, Sheila earned a Masters Degree in English literature from Eastern Michigan University.

Mrs. Cumberworth is employed as a writer by the University of Michigan Medical School. A former English teacher, she has also been a newspaper reporter, freelance writer, and a ghostwriter for three university presidents.

Pastor Daniel V. Biles was born in Philadelphia in 1952. Biles spent his youth in the Philadelphia suburb of King of Prussia, graduating from Upper Merion High School in 1970. He attended Texas Lutheran College in Seguin, Texas, and graduated in 1984. Biles then entered the Lutheran Seminary at Gettysburg. He received his Master of Divinity Degree in May of 1978. He was ordained to the Office of the Word and Sacrament ministry of the Lutheran Church in America on June 11, 1978.

From 1978 to 1985, Biles served as pastor of St. Mark's-Temple Lutheran Church in Cilfton Heights, Pa. During these years he met and married Barbara A. Yarnall, a Lutheran parochial school teacher. The couple has two children, Gretchen Kanthi, born in 1981, and Nathan Baker, born in 1984.

In addition to this publication, Pastor Biles has written two other books. His first, *Pursuing Excellence In Ministry* (Alban Institute, 1988), was recognized as one of the top ten books of 1988 by the Academy of Parish Ministry. His second book, *A Soldier's Journey*, also with Thomas Publications (1990) was an account of his great-grandfather's experiences in the Civil War. Biles has also written numerous articles for theological and journals and religious magazines on theology and the practice of ministry.

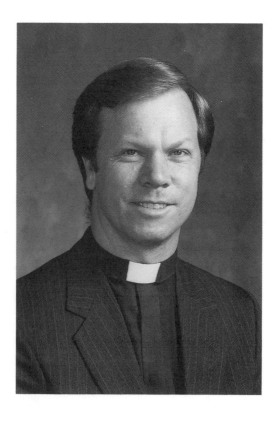

While visiting Fred and Phyllis Lohrum in 1991, Biles met Marianne Swenson and John D'Allesandro, who are also very good friends of Sheila Cumberworth. While conversing about Biles' first Civil War book, Sheila's friends mentioned the existence of the Pierce diaries. Contacts and discussion between Biles and Cumberworth about the diaries and publishing them ensued, and both agreed in short order to write this book as a joint project. Pastor Biles largely researched and wrote the narrative; Sheila Cumberworth transcribed and edited the diaries and final draft.

INDEX